MORE
Polarfleece®
ADVENTURES

Nancy Cornwell

THE JOURNEY CONTINUES...

Krause Publications

700 East State St., Iola, WI 54990-0001
Telephone (715) 445-2214
www.krause.com

Please call or write for our free catalog of publications. Our toll-free number to place an order or obtain a free catalog is 800-258-0929 or please use our regular business telephone 715-445-2214 for editorial comment and further information.

Whenever brand name products are mentioned, it is because I have personally used them and been pleased with the results. In this day and age, with new products being introduced almost daily, there may be other comparable products on the market that will perform the same way.
- Nancy Cornwell

Fine art by Laurie Osborne
Illustrations by Eric Merrill

Printed in the United States of America

Library of Congress Catalog Number: 99-61442

ISBN: 0-87341-791-7

TO MY HUSBAND JEFF

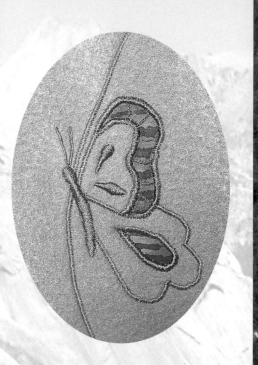

I thank you for

continually encouraging me to spread my wings and expand my horizons.

And for being so supportive when those expanded horizons entail so much time and travel away from our home and our store.

I treasure being your partner in life as well as your partner in business.

ACKNOWLEDGMENTS

When I wrote the first *Adventures* book, it took me almost as long to compose my "thank you" page as it did to write some of the chapters. But this one is easier.

To you, all my sewing friends, old and newly acquainted, I thank you for your tremendous response to my first book. Your excitement, support, and enthusiasm have turned my world delightfully upside-down. Traveling across the nation, presenting seminars, teaching classes, filming television appearances, and giving newspaper interviews. It's been fun. (Rita Farro laughingly says this puts a different spin on the phrase "The Fleecing of America.")

I thank you, my readers and friends, for making the first book such a phenomenal success. And for inspiring this second book.

And I have to especially thank…

Malden Mills for continually creating wonderful new Polarfleece and Polartec fabrics. You set the standard for quality.

Dyersburg Corporation, Menra Mills, Huntingdon Mills, Siltex Mills, Glenoit Mills, and David Textiles for endlessly providing beautiful new patterns, prints, and textures that keep us coming back for more.

Sulky of America for listening to the home sewer and responding with a continual supply of innovative new products and techniques to help us with our creative endeavors. We adventuresome sewers are constantly pushing the limits of what fabrics and machines can do. Thank you, Sulky, for helping us.

Viking Sewing Machine Co., for providing machines and technical support for photography.

To artist Laurie Osborne, illustrator Eric Merrill, photographer Ross Hubbard, book designer Jan Wojtech, and especially editor Barbara Case: You made me look good "in print."

My Stretch & Sew store staff, I Love to Sew friends, and store and mail order customers. They continually support my endeavors, put up with me when I bite off more than I can chew, give me great ideas, and keep the store running while I create, write, travel, and speak. Thank you, ladies. I appreciate you.

My family, who is always there for me.

FOREWORD

Nancy Cornwell just can't leave Polarfleece alone!

To follow her first bestseller, *Adventures With Polarfleece®*, Nancy treats us to a second helping of creative ideas to continue our use and enjoyment of this new age fabric.

So much has gone into the preparation of this book. Nancy's adventures began long before the ink and photos touched these pages. She carefully studied the marketplace, both in fabrics and in ready-to-wear. She searched for the details that make Polarfleece, and garments created from it, unique. Then she figured out the best ways for us to duplicate those details. Her sewing and testing of supplies and notions saves us time and frustration. From her experience, she enthusiastically recommends the best choices.

Just in case you missed her first book, Nancy includes a "refresher course" with basic information about the fabric, needles, stitch length, and more. It's information worth reviewing for success as you try the creative sewing techniques.

Then Nancy's off on new paths with sculpturing and pintucking, two techniques she explores with the new options in this book. Want to sculpture an elegant flower on Polarfleece? The how-tos are here, along with "Nancy's Hints" that provide extra tips and true insights. Once you see all her projects with double needles, you'll gain new appreciation for this pair of needles you used for straight stitching only, or maybe never used at all. Polar ribbing, a distinctive detail easily accomplished with double needles, gives Polarfleece garments the look of expensive ready-to-wear.

And just when you thought cutwork was only for table linens and heirloom sewing, Nancy applies the technique to Polarfleece. You'll discover cutwork to be an easy-but-classy technique with the step-by-step directions, illustrations, and Nancy's collection of designs to use as templates for your own creations.

The style ideas keep coming: appliqué (one of my favorite topics), buttonhole possibilities, zipper treatments, blanket stitching, and lots more. Finally, test your new Polarfleece skills and techniques on Nancy's quick and easy "Scrap Happy" projects at the end of the book.

After so much sewing fun, we can all be glad Nancy Cornwell can't leave Polarfleece alone!

- Mary Mulari
author of *Sweatshirts with Style*
Garments with Style
More Sweatshirts with Style
and *Appliques with Style*

TABLE OF CONTENTS

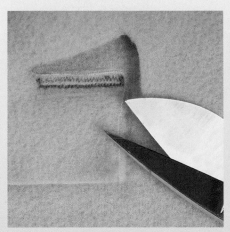

INTRODUCTION

In my first book, *Adventures With Polarfleece®, A Sewing Expedition,* I covered all the basics and tossed in a little bit of playing. The sewing world was so excited to finally have access to the same fabrics found in better ready-to-wear garments that everyone's fingers were itching to learn how to sew these wonderful fabrics.

After reading the first book, everyone found out how easy, fast, and economical fleece garments are to make. Sewers around the country began making vests. Then a few jackets. A hat here and a blanket there. Then they found their families, young and old, asking for "more and more and more!"

In the first book, we played a little. We dabbled with sculpturing. Pintucked a little. Appliquéd a bit. But...

Now it's time to play. *Really play!*

Now it's time to break the rules and take sewing techniques traditionally reserved for tailoring and heirloom sewing applications and use them to create wonderful fleece looks.

Everyone loves make-overs and "before and afters." They show us the possibilities. Use the ideas offered in this book to design and create your own "afters."

Why this book? In my first book, everyone fell in love with sculpturing fleece. It's an easy, fun, and creative way to "imprint" designs on fleece. You can be as simplistic or adventurous as you like. In this book, we'll take sculpturing to different levels. Adding dimension. Using double needles. Sculpturing in free motion. We'll combine sculpturing with other embellishment techniques. And we'll learn new ways to transfer motifs using the newest products on the market.

And...pintucking. You can be practical. Subtle. Or downright overboard! You choose. (The section on polar ribbing is worth its weight in gold!)

Whoever heard of cutwork on fleece? Wait until you see the magnificent looks you can achieve. This isn't about being subtle and understated. This is about knocking their socks off!

This book is written for the adventurer. The sewer who loves sewing with fleece, has made a few garments, and is ready to explore the creative side of fleece and pile fabrics.

Grab your fleece...

Choose your pattern...

Flip through the pages of this book to find ideas and looks that reflect your personality and taste.

Then play... and explore... and experiment...

Add your "personal signature" to every garment you make.

The journey continues.

Learn to view a plain fleece garment...

Love,

Nancy

...as a fresh new canvas awaiting your artistic interpretation. Be subtle or dramatic. Whatever suits your style. Most of all, have fun!

Chapter 1

REFRESHER COURSE

When it comes to digging in and starting to create, sewers are just like little kids. We tend to jump in and sew first, only referring to background information and directions later (and that's only when absolutely necessary). Sewing on fleece and pile fabrics is easy and very forgiving. But there are a few tidbits of background information, basic sewing techniques, and terrific notions that are definitely worth taking the time to review.

This book is titled *More Polarfleece Adventures* because it picks up where my first book left off. In this opening chapter, I offer a quick refresher course on basic fabric and sewing information. See *Adventures With Polarfleece* (my first book, available from Krause Publications) for in-depth sewing techniques, no-fail zipper applications, buttonhole instructions, appropriate pattern choices, ready-to-wear edge finishes, seam options, UltraSuede accents, and designer details.

Fabric Basics

Polarfleece is a well-known, high quality, highly respected trademarked fleece manufactured by Malden Mills. Although incorrect, the term "polarfleece" has been used generically, referring to fleece in general. Polarfleece and Polartec are trademarked fleece names.

There are many mills and manufacturers who offer a wide variety of fleece and pile fabric styles and qualities. The highest quality fleeces are made in the United States and Canada. Malden Mills, Dyersburg Corp., Glenoit, and Menra Mills are the primary United States fleece and pile fabric providers. Siltex Mills and Huntingdon Mills are Canadian companies who offer high quality goods. Many fleeces are manufactured and imported from the Orient. Most of them are inferior quality, imported to be sold at discount, and will not perform to the discriminating

The blue is Berber, the bears are plush, and the berry is fleece.

sewer's standards. My favorite imported fleece is manufactured for and imported by David Textiles.

Adventures With Polarfleece offers a detailed explanation of the different types of fleece and pile fabrics on the market, the brand names manufactured by the various companies, along with which fleeces the ready-to-wear brand name manufacturers use. It also addresses the many differences between fleece and pile fabrics, how and where to use them, and what characteristics they possess.

Most of the fleeces pictured in this book are mid-weight, double-sided (fuzzy on both sides), with a sheared even finish. Berbers have a bumpy, lambswool appearance on one side with a flat knit underside. Plush fabrics are like short velvety fur on one side with a flat knit underside. Berbers and plushes are pile fabrics, referring to the method used in their construction.

Generally speaking, fleece is made from 100% polyester fibers and pile fabrics are made from a blend of acrylic and polyester fibers. Polyester and acrylic fibers are hydrophobic by nature, meaning they "hate" and retain very little water. That's why they work so well for outerwear.

Fleece and pile fabrics don't run, ravel, or shrink, so you can enjoy the luxury of skipping the pretreating step. You can buy the fabric and immediately cut it out and start sewing! (If you are a longtime sewer, this feels like sinning. After so many years of being preached to about the importance of first pretreating your fabric, skipping this step feels delightfully naughty!)

Usually when I refer to "fleece", I am including fleece and pile fabrics. I will note it when a technique is not suitable for Berber or plush fabrics.

Fabric & Garment Care

Laundering

To avoid unnecessary abrasion, launder fleece garments inside out, separately or with similar garments. Use a powdered detergent and launder in a lukewarm wash on the gentle cycle.

Note: Liquid detergents can alter the effectiveness of the moisture wicking chemical treatment applied to

Nancy's Disclaimer

There will be times throughout the book when I instruct you to iron a stabilizer to the wrong side of the fleece so you can do specific techniques. Iron with a light touch. The iron should never come in contact with the fleece, but only touch the stabilizer.

some lighter weight fleeces.

Do not use bleach, dryer softener sheets, or water softeners. Softeners have an adverse effect on the Durable Water Repellant (DWR) chemical finish that is applied to the surface of some mid- and heavy-weight fleeces.

Pressing

Pressing is not necessary or recommended. If, during the construction stage, pressing seems necessary, hold the iron above the fabric and apply steam. Then gently finger press to encourage the fleece to lay in the desired position. Never place an iron directly on the fabric. Direct contact may leave a permanent imprint or melt the fabric. Since fleece and pile fabrics are made from manmade fibers, if the loft is flattened by heat, it cannot be revived.

The Eternal Question: Which Is the Right Side?

It's important to know which is the right side (the face) of the fabric because that is the side that will wear better and look nicer for a longer period of time. If there was a finishing treatment or added shearing step, it would have been done to the face of the fabric. Some fleeces are non-pill on one side only. If a water-repellent finish was applied, you want to make sure that side ends up facing the weather.

On pile fabrics, with their novelty face and plain knitted underside, it's easy to tell the right from the wrong side. Single-sided fleeces, with their fuzzy face and knit back, are easy to tell. Double-sided fleeces are not always so easy.

Rule of Thumb: Fleece fabrics curl to the right side when pulled along the selvage edges and curl to the wrong side when stretched on the crossgrain.

Occasional Exceptions: If I choose a print fleece that is much prettier on one side than the other, I use the side with the crisper, cleaner print. (If the selvage edge also curls towards the attractive side, so much the better!)

I test for water repellency by pouring water on both sides of the fleece. If it beads up better on one side than

Nancy's Golden Rule

After you've determined which is the right side of the fleece, be religious and meticulous about marking the right side on every garment piece you cut out. For added convenience, be consistent about where you place your marks (saves later hunt-and-search time). These marking steps will save confusion and possible errors when you sit down to sew. Chacopel pencils are a good choice for marking your fabric.

the other, I declare the beaded side the right side.

If I bought a bargain piece and I'm a little nervous about how it will perform, I "rough it up" for a preview of how it will wear. I rub the fabric against itself on both sides and examine which is a little worse for wear. That will be the wrong side.

Pretreat it. I know I just said that it's not necessary to pretreat fleeces for shrinkage or color bleeding. However, I know that both sides of the fleece react differently to laundering. If I were making a color-blocked garment from an assortment of fleeces, I would first pretreat the fleeces to compare the appearance on both sides of each fabric before sewing them together.

Sewing Basics

Sewing Machine & Serger

Make sure the machines you are about to use are clean, oiled, and in good working order. When finished sewing, clean and oil your machines. Sewing with fleece results in a lot of accumulated lint which absorbs oil.

Fleeces can easily be sewn on a conventional sewing machine or a serger. The following thread, needle, and stitch length guidelines apply to both.

Thread

Choose good quality, long staple polyester thread to match your fabric, or a shade darker. This is not the time to hassle with bargain threads that will knot and fray.

Needles

Always begin a project with a fresh, new needle.

Because fleece is a knitted fabric, choose a universal, stretch, or ballpoint needle. These needles have rounded or softened points that deflect rather than pierce the yarns.

Choose the needle *size* according to the *weight* of the fleece. Use the smallest size needle possible that is strong enough for the job.

Recommended sizes:
　　Lightweight fleece - 70/10 or 75/11
　　Mid-weight fleece - 80/12 or 90/14
　　Heavyweight fleece - 100/16

Nancy's Troubleshooting Tip

If your thread snags and breaks, and…
　　you are using good quality thread
　　you changed to a fresh needle
　　your machine is in good working order…
Check for rough spots by examining:
　　the needle opening on the throat plate
　　the hook
　　the presser foot opening
　　the presser foot soleplate.
During the course of everyday sewing, we break needles. For whatever reason, occasional needle breakage is a fact of life. A needle breaks because it came in contact with something hard - probably one of the items listed above. When the needle hits and breaks, it frequently results in roughed, gouged areas. Any rough, nicked areas can snag and break thread.

To check for rough spots, use an old nylon or some other "easily snaggable" fabric and rub it over the areas of concern.

*Use crocus cloth (available from a hardware store) and **very gently** polish the rough spot. If the rough area is deeply gouged, take the machine to your dealer. If you file it too much, you may interfere with the stitch formation.*

If you notice a lot of gouges around the needle opening on the throat plate, take it to your dealer. It may be time to replace the throat plate.

But (there's always a but), if the sewing conditions change, then the rules change! If you are sewing on a mid-weight fleece using a size 90/14 needle, and all of a sudden you have an area where you are stitching through three or four layers, then you must change to a larger size needle. The medium size needle handled the medium weight fleece under normal conditions, but the added weight and bulk of multiple layers may cause the needle to bend and skip stitches or break. When the conditions change, the needle size requirements change too.

Choose the needle *type* according to the "fussiest" element of your sewing. If you are applying UltraSuede trim or appliqué onto fleece, you would alter your needle choice to fit the demands of UltraSuede. UltraSuede is fussier than fleece and sews nicer with a stretch needle. If topstitching on UltraSuede with metallic thread, choose a needle type to accommodate the metallic thread. Because metallic thread is fussier than UltraSuede and fussier than fleece, you should choose a metallic needle for best stitch quality.

Stitch Length

In garment construction, use the fewest number of stitches possible to be functional in the garment you are making. As a rule, this is seven to nine stitches per inch, or approximately a 3mm to 3.5mm stitch length. This length is appropriate for most loose-fitting fleece garments with no high stress seams.

Troubleshooting: If your machine balks at feeding the fleece, first try lengthening the stitch length. If more help is needed, lighten the pressure on the presser foot.

Note: A stitch length that is too short tends to stretch the fleece. Rippled seams or fanned edges are signs of a too-short stitch length.

In close fitting garments that require the seams to give, shorten the stitch length to 12 to 14 stitches per inch or a 2mm to 2.5mm stitch length. The additional stitches are needed for more strength for high stress seams. In the relaxed state, these seams may appear rippled but they will be smooth when stretched to fit the body.

Serger Tidbits

Stitch Choice: Use a three/four thread serger seam.
Cutting Width: Move the cutting blade to the left to cut off more fabric. This relieves the jam-packing of heavier fleece in the narrow seam allowance.
Differential Feed: To keep the seams laying flat on fleeces with more stretch, adjust the differential as necessary to 1 or 1.5.

Gotta-Have Notions

I mention the following products throughout the book because I have used them and have been pleased with their performance. There may be similar products available that will also work.

Adventures With Polarfleece®
by Nancy Cornwell

I am obviously biased, but this book is acknowledged to be the sewing industry's "polar encyclopedia." This polar resource book is where you'll find all the information you need about fleece and pile fabrics, including in-depth fabric information (from technical information to which fabric to use where); sewing machine and serger techniques; what to look for in patterns; seam options; ready-to-wear edges finishes;

no-hassle zipper applications ranging from practical everyday zippers to designer applications; buttonholes (standard, fashion, and troubleshooting); UltraSuede accents; introduction to sculpturing and texturing fleece; plus projects to sew.

Wash-A-Way Wondertape
1/4" Double-Sided Basting Tape by Collins

I continually refer to this product in both of my books because it can be used in so many ways. I choose this product because the 1/4" width has terrific holding power, you can sew through it without gumming up the needle, and because it doesn't need to be removed - it launders away!

It's perfect for holding garment pieces in place where pins would be awkward and it is the only way to "baste" zippers and pockets in place. It also spot holds appliqués and trims in place.

Although Wondertape doesn't gum up the needle in normal sewing, if you are applying yards and yards of "taped" trim, you may eventually experience a sticky needle. To remove buildup, simply wipe the needle clean with rubbing alcohol.

Long Glass Head Pins

Since pins can easily be lost in the loft of the fabric,

choose longer pins. For best visibility (thus avoiding unwanted contact with serger blades), pin at a 90° angle to the seamline or cut edges.

Chacopel Pencils from Clover

Chacopel pencils are fabric marking pencils. They are my favorite because they mark easily on fleece and stay marked until I rub out the marks. Don't over-sharpen. Sharpen to a medium point, not a fine point. A fine point will break too easily.

Totally Stable

Totally Stable is a temporary iron-on tear-away stabilizer from Sulky. I use it to stabilize fleeces for sculpturing and cutwork and for transferring designs.

Use a dry iron when pressing to adhere. The stabilizer will remain in the stitches, so use it only when the underside of the work will not be visible. Totally Stable is available in white or black.

Nancy's Hints

#1 *When adhering Totally Stable, remember that this is only a temporary stage. Set the iron temperature appropriately for the fabric used. Use only enough heat, time, and pressure to adhere the stabilizer. If the iron is too hot or if you over-press, the hold will be too strong. The stabilizer will then be difficult to remove and you also risk "defleecing" the fabric. It's better to under-press and go back to touch up as necessary.*

#2 *When removing any tear-away stabilizer, place one hand along the stitches and with the other hand, tear at a 45° angle to the stitching line. Imagine the age-old direction, "tear along the dotted line." This will prevent roughness and possible distortion of the stitches.*

#3 *Another easy way to remove Totally Stable is to use a pointed object (like serger tweezers, seam ripper end, small sewing machine screwdriver) and score the Totally Stable alongside the stitches. This scoring releases the hold and allows easy removal.*

Solvy

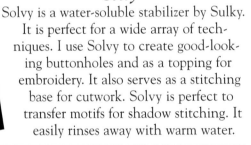

Solvy is a water-soluble stabilizer by Sulky. It is perfect for a wide array of techniques. I use Solvy to create good-looking buttonholes and as a topping for embroidery. It also serves as a stitching base for cutwork. Solvy is perfect to transfer motifs for shadow stitching. It easily rinses away with warm water.

Nancy's Hints

#1 *When tracing a design on Solvy, use a water erase marker, air erase marker, or fine-line permanent pen. If using a pen, make sure it's permanent ink. That way, when rinsed away, the permanent ink adheres only to the Solvy rather than transferring to the fabric.*

#2 *If I am going to be stitching over Solvy traced with permanent ink, I choose an ink color to match the thread color. That way, if it takes more than one rinsing to entirely remove the Solvy, any visible ink blends in with the stitching.*

#3 *Pay careful attention to the KK2000 Caution #3 that follows about using KK2000 with Solvy.*

Sulky's KK2000 Temporary Adhesive Spray

This innovative product is the answer to many "sticky" situations. It is used extensively throughout this book to make a wide variety of applications and techniques much easier. The beauty of this spray adhesive is that it absorbs into the fibers in two to three days and completely disappears in three to ten days! (The timing depends on the amount sprayed, fabric type, heat, and humidity conditions.) The simple explanation: the molecular structure breaks down, not allowing the chemicals, glue, and propellant to harden. There will be absolutely no residue remaining on the fabric.

This heavier-than-air propellant is not petroleum based, so it is not flammable. Because the spray is heavy, you can hold the can as close as 6" to 10" from your fabric. It goes exactly where you want it without wasteful over-spray. And it is environmentally friendly!

Note: KK2000 is not water-soluble. It does not wash out. Pay close attention to Caution #3 below.

Important KK2000 Caution #1: Spray KK2000 on the surface that will be removed rather than on the fleece.

Example: Lightly spray the KK2000 adhesive on the stabilizer and then adhere the fleece. Or lightly spray the adhesive on the Solvy and then adhere the fleece. When the stabilizer or the Solvy is removed, most of the adhesive will be removed with it, leaving only a trace amount on the fleece (which disappears over time).

Important KK2000 Caution #2: Spray lightly. KK2000 has terrific holding power and doesn't need to be heavily applied. Excessive adhesive takes much longer to disappear.

Important KK2000 Caution #3: KK2000 dissolves and goes away on its own. Any interference with its natural process risks a gummy result that will be difficult to remove. Don't try to wash it out - it's not water-soluble.

Example: In some techniques I spray Solvy with KK2000 adhesive and adhere it to the fleece. Although Solvy rinses away with warm water, if you rinse the Solvy-adhered fleece, you will get a gummy residue (because KK2000 is not water-soluble). It is important to first peel off the adhesive-sprayed Solvy. The little bits remaining in the stitches won't present a problem when rinsed away. It is still best to allow time for the remaining hint of adhesive to disappear.

Important KK2000 Caution #4: Machine manufacturers recommend that when applying spray adhesives, you work in an area totally removed from your conventional sewing machine, serger, and embroidery machine. This precautionary step ensures that no adhesive comes in contact with the tension discs or any other sensitive machine mechanism. Better safe than sorry!

Snap Source Sport Snaps

These sport snaps are the perfect alternative to zippers or buttons and button-

holes. I prefer this brand because they have longer prongs for better gripping power. They easily handle two layers of mid-

weight fleece. There are a variety of sizes available, with sizes 20 and 24 being the most popular choices for use on fleece. The SnapSetter tool offers an easy and accurate method for applying snaps to the garment.

Nancy's Caution

Don't apply post-style snaps to fleece unless they are affixed to woven fabric trim. Post-style snaps are designed for woven fabrics, while prong-style snaps are designed for knit fabrics. (For a thorough understanding of how and where to use all types of sport snaps, refer to the book It's A Snap! written by industry expert Jeanine Twigg.)

Rotary Cutters

Rotary cutters are available from several companies. Bulky fleeces are much easier to cut when using the larger size 60mm cutter. The larger blade effortlessly handles the bulk while the corresponding

larger handle is comfortable to use. (I now use the larger blade for all my rotary cutting needs.) Choose the medium 45mm rotary cutter with a wave blade or pinking blade when you want a decorative blunt edge finish.

Sweater Combs

It's easy to freshen tired looking fleece with a simple little tool called a sweater comb. Coats & Clark offers the Fuzz Away (pictured here). Collins offers the D-Fuzz-It. These clever notions feature a fine rough edge that removes pills, lint, and fuzz from the surface of the fabric without roughing up the fleece. I use them to freshen any fabric.

An Important Word About Adhesives

The following information applies to all arenas of sewing, not just fleece. Learn the principles of adhesives and you will avoid problems when it is time to remove them.

Tacky Adhesives

The chemical makeup and design of a tacky adhesive causes the hold to become stronger the longer it is in place. Imagine cellophane tape placed on a window. If peeled off in one minute it comes off quite easily, but if you wait a day or two the job is not so easy. This same basic principle applies to tacky adhesives used in sewing.

Tear-Away Stabilizers, Films, Tapes

The longer these products are in place, the stronger the hold. If an adhesive is used as a temporary aid that will later be removed by tearing or rinsing away, the removal process will be much easier if there is a short time span between adhering and removing.

Remember and apply this principle to save many unnecessary hours of tedious picking and removing of adhesive stabilizers.

Chapter 2

SCULPTURING & BEYOND

Sculpturing on Polarfleece is a fun easy embellishment technique that allows you to add personality to your fleece garments. You can create "prints," etch personalized motifs, and coordinate prints and solids. No longer are there just plain fleeces, now there are more fresh canvases to work on!

Sculpturing is easy to do. Simply put, it's satin stitching on fleece. The stitch sinks into the loft of the fleece and creates a groove. That groove imprints designs, patterns, and motifs. The fleece looks engraved or etched. You can be as understated or as dramatic as you like.

Sculpturing is done with the feed dogs up, just like stitching an appliqué. Sculpturing is satin stitching in a continuous design, a motif, outlining a print, or simply meandering. As you work your way through this chapter, you'll find a variety of ways to enhance fleece with sculpturing. Use these ideas as a springboard to develop your own creations.

First introduced in *Adventures With Polarfleece,* sculpturing quickly became everyone's favorite technique. In this book, we'll start with the basics of sculpturing then expand into new territory, employing new products and new techniques.

What You Need to Get Started

Pattern

Choose a pattern that will be complemented by a contrast sculptured yoke, sleeves, collar, pocket, inset, lapel, etc. Or sculpture a simple motif on a plain front pullover to imitate expensive ready-mades. Sculpturing can be done anywhere on a garment as long as the underside will not show (because the stabilizer remains visible in the stitching). However, if you absolutely must have sculpturing in an area where the underside will be visible, see the stabilizing alternative on page 20.

Fabric

Sculpturing looks best on fleece and Berber fabrics. Sculpturing doesn't show well on plush fabrics. Buy yardage according to pattern requirements. Sculpturing doesn't require more yardage.

Cutting: Sculpturing is done on cutout garment pieces before construction. Unlike many embellishment techniques, sculpturing doesn't alter the fabric's dimensions. Therefore, you can sculpt on cutout yokes, pockets, sleeves, etc.

Needle Threads

Depending on how much sculpturing will be done, you will need a minimum of two or more spools of thread for the needle. Following is a list of thread choices, the effects they offer, and important usage information.

Regular Thread: Use for construction and possibly for sculpturing when you can't find a suitable rayon color. The effect is very subtle, giving shadowed grooves.

Rayon Thread: This is the most popular choice because it lends a lovely sheen to the grooves. Choose a shade darker for a tone-on-tone effect or a strong contrast for dramatic appeal. Use with an embroidery needle.

Use one of the many sculpturing ideas presented in this chapter to put your "signature" on an ordinary garment

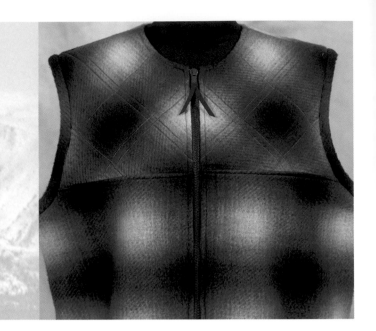

Nancy's Hint

When sculpturing the blue plaid tunic vest, I had a hard time finding the right thread color to complement the heathered colors. Navy was too dull, royal was too bright. Medium and lighter blues just didn't work. Suddenly it dawned on me: Why not combine two colors? Royal and navy? Perfect! The result was a tweedy effect that complemented the print perfectly!

To use two threads, thread the machine as you would for double-needle sewing, except run both threads through the same eye of a single needle. Choose a larger size needle to accommodate the extra thread bulk.

Metallic Thread: The glitter offers a subtle sparkle in the grooves. Choose high quality thread. Metallic thread may be a little temperamental to use, so be gentle and follow the rules. Use a metallic needle and sew at medium speed (embellishing with metallic thread is not a pedal-to-the-metal operation). Using a needle lubricant may be helpful.

Note: Although metallic needles come in size 80, you will have better luck and less thread breakage using a size 90.

If metallic thread breaks continually:

a) change to a larger size needle

b) check for rough spots on your needle plate, hook, and shuttle race

c) if the thread is older, the outer layers may be dry and brittle (exposure to sunshine and dust deteriorate thread). Pull off a few yards, discard the outer layers, and try again.

Variegated Thread: This type of thread creates interesting striped effects.

Clear or Smoke Thread: Use this when outline sculpturing a print for a quilted effect. It's perfect to use on a multicolored print with no predominant color to accent. Use a size 80/12 needle and loosen the needle tension quite a bit.

Bobbin Thread

You'll need two or more spools of regular thread to match the fabric color. Lightweight bobbin thread may also be used in the bobbin when sculpturing.

Needles

➜ Choose a size 90/14 universal needle for construction and regular thread.

➜ Choose a size 90/14 embroidery needle for rayon thread.

➜ Choose a size 90/14 metallic needle for metallic thread.

➜ Choose a size 80/12 universal for clear thread.

Needle Lubricant

This is helpful if you are having difficulty with metallic thread.

Sulky Totally Stable
(iron-on tear-away stabilizer)

You'll need enough yardage to back all the areas that are to be sculptured.

Why iron-on stabilizer? Most fleeces have quite a bit of stretch in at least one direction. To prevent distortion, it is imperative to remove the stretch factor from the fabric before beginning stitching.

Nancy's Caution

When adhering Totally Stable, remember that this is only a temporary stage. Set the iron temperature on the cooler, rather than hotter side. Use only enough heat, time, and pressure to adhere the stabilizer. If the iron is too hot or if you over-press, the hold will be too strong. If this happens, the stabilizer will be difficult to remove and you risk de-fleecing your fabric. It is better to under-press and touch up as necessary.

A pin-on stabilizer, being a separate layer, would allow the fleece to stretch as the satin stitching is worked. The iron-on stabilizer adhered to the fleece becomes one with the fabric and doesn't allow the fabric to stretch during stitching.

Sulky Solvy

This water-soluble stabilizer is used to transfer designs or motifs onto fleece fabric. It's also used with KK2000 adhesive as a stabilizer backing when the wrong side of sculpturing will be visible.

Sulky KK2000

This temporary spray adhesive is used to adhere stabilizer to fleece.

Nancy's Hint

For best results, spray the adhesive on the stabilizer, not the fleece. Remember: spray the adhesive on what you will be removing, not what will remain. That way, most of the adhesive is removed when the stabilizer is discarded.

Things to Think About

Before sculpturing an area, determine if there are any design elements in the garment that need to be considered.

Will There Be Buttonholes?

Before sculpturing an area that will have button-holes, mark all the buttonhole placements so the sculpturing stitches completely avoid the buttonholes. This applies to the facings as well as the garment front.

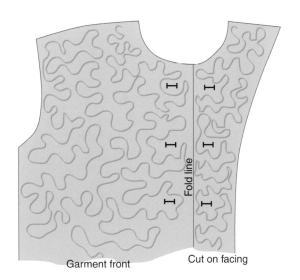

Garment front   Cut on facing

Will There Be Folded Edges?

If doing a free-style meandering design, stitching over a fold line may result in an uneven dimpled edge. Draw in a cut-on facing fold line, pocket fold line, collar fold line, etc. and avoid meandering across the line. Sculpturing lines in a geometric, even gridded design may cross a garment fold line and still look symmetrical. Uneven meandering lines may look uneven.

No Facing on a Sculptured Yoke?

If the garment has a zip front that may be worn open and turned back, be aware that Totally Stable will remain in the stitches and be visible. Since there will be no facing to hide the wrong side, either line the garment or use Solvy as the stabilizer (refer to the stabilizing alternative on page 20).

Rollback Cuffs

A roll-up cuff is a nice sleeve finish when the fleece doesn't have an obvious right or wrong side, but be aware that the wrong side of the fabric will be the visible side of the cuff. This means you will stabilize on the right side and sculpture stitch on the wrong side of the fabric (opposite of other sculpturing applications).

Garment Design Elements

When deciding on the placement of sculpturing lines, take into account any garment construction details that may interfere with the design. Be aware of seamlines, topstitching, neck trimming, collar rollback or turnover, zippers, etc.

Sculpturing Basics

There are only four basic steps to sculpturing. Of course, adventuresome sewers always come up with a million alternatives. So, let's first start with the basics, then expand into an array of variables.

1. Cut out the garment sections to be sculptured. Remember that sculpturing is done on cutout garment pieces *before* construction and on a single layer of fabric only. If there is a facing, sculpture the facing separately.

2. Iron Totally Stable to the wrong side of the garment, behind areas that are to be sculptured. Use a dry iron, appropriate temperature, and light pressure. Do not touch the iron to the fleece.

3. Satin stitch the design. Satin stitch the sculpturing lines on the right side of the fleece using a 3.5mm to 4mm zigzag width and a shorter stitch length. This is not quite a tight satin stitch density. A hint of fabric should show between the stitches. Loosen the needle thread tension as necessary so the needle thread pulls slightly to the underside.

4. Remove and discard the stabilizer. Couldn't be much easier!

Nancy's Note

Always stitch a test sample to determine the stitch width, stitch density, and tension adjustment. It's worth a few extra minutes to get the look just right.

Stabilizing Alternative

Stabilizing the fleece with Totally Stable iron-on tear-away stabilizer results in stabilizer remaining visible in the stitches on the underside. But what happens when the sculpturing underside will be exposed and you don't want the stabilizer to show?

In that case, use Solvy as the stabilizer instead of Totally Stable. Spray KK2000 on the Solvy and adhere it to the wrong side of the fleece, behind areas that are to be sculptured. When finished sculpturing, peel away the Solvy and discard. Allow the adhesive to disappear on its own.

The Wide World of Sculpturing

There are so many ways to play with the sculpturing technique. Stitch all-over freeform designs, large and small motifs, gridded and planned designs, even double-needle and free-motion sculpturing! What follows here is a wide variety of sculpturing ideas, techniques, and how-to's. When dreaming up ideas of your own, thumb through these ideas to develop your own plan of attack.

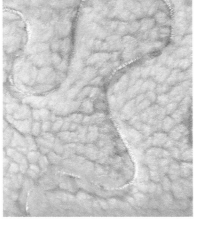

Meandering

Meandering is a fast and easy way to sculpture. There is no need to draw a design. Simply wander as you stitch, creating jigsaw-puzzle-piece shapes. As you stitch, think hills and valleys, harbors and peninsulas. Avoid crossing over previous meandering stitching lines. Sew in one long continuous "squiggle" line. If you become locked in a corner, stop, tie off the thread tails on the underside and begin again.

Not every nook and cranny is supposed to be identical! Don't worry if the stitch density varies around larger and smaller curves. Wait until you are finished before criticizing your work. The whole looks great, even if some of the parts may be imperfect.

Nancy's Hint

When you meander, stitch in an open, flowing pattern, especially on larger garment sections. If you sew in tight little intricate curves, you will find yourself sitting at the machine for an inordinate length of time, using tons of thread. Plus, a tight design doesn't allow the area between the sculpture lines to puff and give dimension. A sample stitching before you begin will give you all the necessary information you need to "wander."

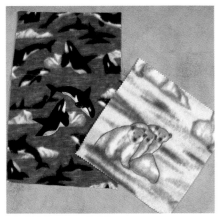

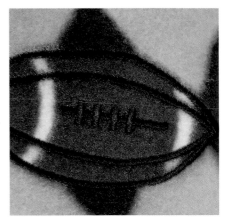

Outline sculpturing brings a print to life.

Football printed fleece "before" sculpturing.

Football printed fleece "after" sculpturing with black rayon thread.

Outline Sculptured Quilted Look

Sue Mitrovich loved this sports motif in the perfect school colors. Combining the warmth of fleece with dramatic sculpturing makes this vest a winner every time!

Choose a printed fleece. Sculpture the fleece by satin stitch outlining the dominant print lines. Outline sculpturing results in a soft quilted appearance. When an entire garment is created from a print, consider outline stitching just a couple areas for a subtle contrast. Yokes, inset panels, shoulder areas, collars, or pockets are great places to "quilt."

If the print lines offer a dominant color, choose that color thread to enhance the design.

If the print is multicolored and one thread color will interfere with the print, use clear or smoke thread for the sculpture stitching. This results in a subtle grooved look with no color change.

Decorative Stitches

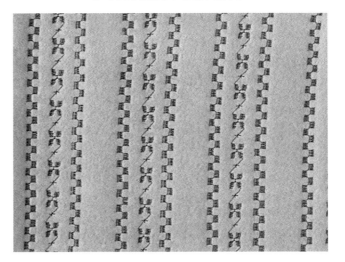

Instead of using a plain zigzag satin stitch for the sculpturing lines, try a simple decorative satin stitch on your machine. Don't pick an intricate multi-motion open design, but rather a simple straightforward shape like a wave, diamond, scallop, dot, heart, etc. You want it to be a fill-in satin stitch pattern so it will show when it sinks into the fleece. If you choose a multi-motion intricate open stitch pattern, you will spend a lot of time stitching without a dramatic end result.

Geometric Designs – Gridded Lines & Planned Patterns

This is great idea when you want a coordinate solid and "print" fleece. You make your own print. You can have a solid body with a matching diamond print yoke or a solid jacket with box check sleeves. For the adventuresome, create a plaid. You are only limited by your imagination.

As always, cut out your garment pieces, then stabilize those pieces that are to be sculptured with Totally Stable.

There are two ways to attack drawing and sewing the grid lines - the hard way and the easy way.

The Hard Way

Using a Clover Chacopel pencil or fabric marker and a see-through ruler, draw all the sculpturing lines. Then cover all the drawn lines with satin stitching.

The Easy Way (the only way to go!)

Use a Clover Chacopel pencil or fabric marker to draw only the first sculpturing line and satin stitch the line.

Attach a quilting bar to the presser foot (your machine brand may call it an edge guide or spacer bar and may attach to the presser foot or to the presser foot shank). Move the guide the desired distance from the needle for your next sculpturing stitching line.

Using the quilt bar as a guide, continue sewing lines until the fabric piece is completely sculpture stitched.

If you are creating squares or boxes, use a Chacopel pencil and a see-through ruler to draw a second line that intersects the first row at a 90° angle.

Again using the quilting bar, stitch the remaining intersecting lines until the fabric is completely covered. Quick and easy!

If you want the design to be diamond shapes, when drawing the second line, simply slide the ruler at different angles until you find a pleasing angle for the diamond shape. Use the quilt bar to finish sculpturing the fleece.

Matching Geometric Gridded Designs

When sculpturing gridded geometric designs such as diamonds, squares, plaids, etc., match the sculpture lines the same way you would handle a plaid or a stripe.

For example, if you are sculpturing a garment that requires you to match the sculpturing lines on a right and left yoke…

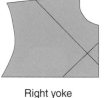

Right yoke   Left yoke

1. Cut out and stabilize both the left and right front yokes.

2. Lay the yokes alongside each other and draw the first base line. Mirror image the right and left while aligning at the center front.

3. Draw the second intersecting line, again mirror imaging and matching at the center front.

Geometric Designs With Flair

Following the same premise as outlined above for sculpturing boxes and squares or diamond designs, you can easily take a couple small steps forward and add a touch of panache to your design.

Wavy Lines

Who says that boxes and diamonds can only be made with straight lines? Add softness and a feminine touch by curving the base grid lines. For even more interest, sculpture stitch the curved lines with a decorative stitch! Looks difficult, but it is stitched the same as the planned and gridded designs.

Nancy's Hint

If you are sculpturing wavy lines on more than one garment piece, an easy way to match the waves is to first draw the wavy line on a piece of paper. Then cut along the waved edge and use it as a template to trace the first line on each garment piece.

Making Your Own Print

Stitch the decorative satin stitch sculptured lines in a wavy grid design. When finished, choose a simple single decorative motif on your machine and center the motifs in the wavy blocks to create an all-over print design.

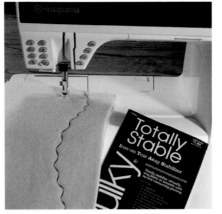

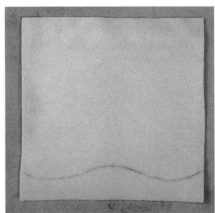

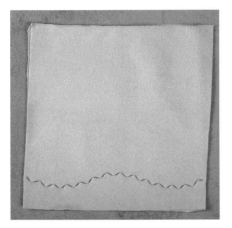

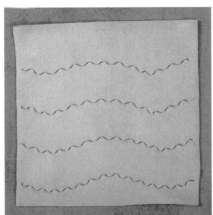

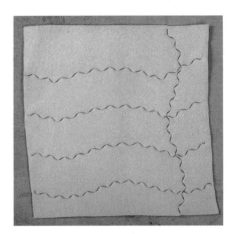

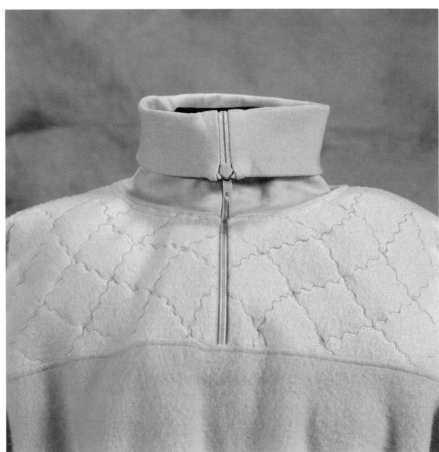

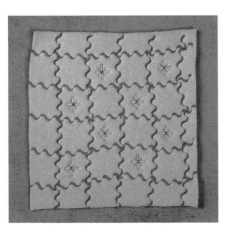

Combining Sculpturing & Pintucks

Stitch the sculptured lines on stabilized fleece. Remove the stabilizer. Change to a double needle and add rows of pintucking (refer to the Pintucking chapter).

Nancy's Caution

Combining different embellishment techniques is definitely one of those times when you need to "plan first and sew second." Combining sculpturing and pintucks is a good case study. For sculpturing, the fleece must be stabilized, but for pintucking you need unstabilized fleece so the welts can raise. If you pintuck first, then press Totally Stable on the fleece to stabilize it for sculpturing, you'll flatten the pintucks. If you pintuck on stabilized fleece, the pintuck welts won't raise.

So...

1. *Stabilize the fleece with Totally Stable.*
2. *Sculpture your design.*
3. *Remove the stabilizer.*
4. *Pintuck.*

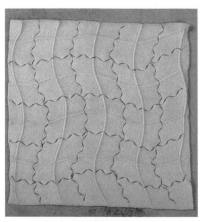

When combining techniques, pay close attention to the order of techniques. Stabilize. Sculpture. Remove the stabilizer. Pintuck. The shawl collar edge above is finished with the cheaters's wrapped edge from Adventures With Polarfleece.

Double Needle Sculpturing

What happens when you sculpture with double needles? You get double sculpturing - a classy look with twice the fun! Twin satin stitch lines snuggled against each other offer a totally different effect.

Thread Color Choices

1. Same color on both needles for a bold statement - a great way to coordinate with a contrast zipper, ribbing, or trim.
2. Different color thread in each needle for a fun way to play with colors. Lots of choices. Strong contrast. Sporty. Ombre effect.

3. Blend colors with fleece for an understated appearance.

Double Needle Sculpture Testing & Sample Stitching

As always, before trying a new technique for real, it's smart to stitch some test samples to adjust needle tension, stitch length and width, and to determine what you like.

1. Stabilize a scrap piece of fleece with Totally Stable.
2. Insert 2.0 double needles and thread the needles with rayon thread. (Refer to page 39 for directions.) Leave regular thread in the bobbin.

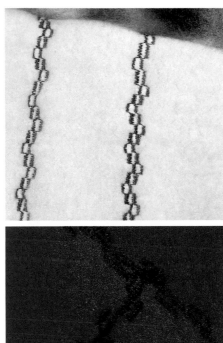

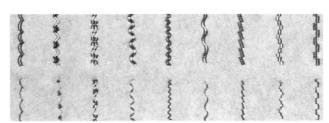

To see the creative potential of various simple satin stitches, make a stitch sampler. The stitches on the bottom are sewn using a single needle. The stitches on the top are the same designs stitched with a double needle.

3. Set the machine stitch width to accommodate 2.0 double needles. *Note:* I chose 2.0 double needles because combined with a 2.5mm stitch width, they provide a very pretty finished stitch width and stitch pattern alignment. The resulting stitches are noticeable without being heavy and overpowering. They touch nicely, side-by-side.

To determine the widest possible zigzag width without breaking a needle, you will need to do a little math. Add .5mm to the needle separation (2.0 + .5 = 2.5mm), then subtract this number from the maximum stitch width available on your machine.

a) If you have a 5mm machine, 2.5mm will be the maximum width allowable.

b) If you have a 4mm machine, 1.5mm will be the maximum width allowable. A little narrower, but still lovely.

c) If your machine offers wider than a 5mm stitch width, choosing a wider width will probably result in gaps between the stitching rows. You might like to experiment with a 2.5 or 3.0 double needle combined with the wider stitch width. Experimentation will determine what look you like.

d) Refer to the stitch width chart on page 38.

e) If you have a computerized machine, engage the double needle function for the size double needle you are using. The machine will automatically engage this safety feature and not allow you to choose a too-wide stitch width.

4. Test a variety of stitches on your machine. First do a simple zigzag satin stitch, then try simple fill-in decorative satin stitches on your machine. Avoid open stitches since they won't show very well. Loosen the needle tension so the rayon threads pull slightly to the underside.

Nancy's Hint

Try a wide variety of stitches. You'll be surprised at which ones look terrific and just as surprised at which ones don't!

After deciding on a decorative stitch, experiment with turning corners. Since the 2.0 double needles are narrow and fleece is forgiving, you can pivot and turn the corner in the usual way (sink needles, pivot, and turn). However, you may want to try a couple corners to determine exactly where in the stitch you want to pivot.

Nancy's Hint

If you have a computerized machine, refer to your manual and take advantage of these functions: pattern begin, half pattern, pattern end, and needle down.

Garment Idea:
Double Needle Sculptured Pullover

You Will Need

➔ Your favorite plain front pullover sweatshirt style pattern
➔ Fleece per pattern requirements (not suitable for Berber or plush fabrics)
➔ Notions per pattern requirements
➔ 2 spools rayon thread (for sculpturing)
➔ 2.0/75 or 2.0/80 embroidery double needle
➔ Chacopel pencil
➔ Totally Stable (iron-on tear-away stabilizer)
➔ Pattern tracing material

Pattern Drafting

1. Trace one whole garment on pattern tracing material. (If different neckline choices are available, trace the neckline for a crew neck for correct sculpture line placement. The neckline style can be changed after the sculpture design lines are drawn.)

2. To draw design lines for double needle sculpturing on the *pattern* front:

a) Draw in the center front line.

b) Draw a horizontal line across the front, 1" below the armscye point.

c) Measure the shoulder length from the crew neck edge to the armhole. Mark a dot at the midpoint of both shoulder edges.

d) Draw the first V from the shoulder dots to the center front line, ending on the horizontal line.

e) Draw the second V on the right front (as when wearing) 2" to 3½" from the first V lines (2" for smaller sizes, 3" for medium sizes, 3½" for larger sizes).

f) Draw the third V on the left front, same as in step e above.

g) Draw a center diamond, 1" to 2" away from and surrounding the middle diamond.

Construction

1. Cut out the front, back, and sleeves according to the pattern directions.

2. Stabilize the fleece for sculpture stitching by pressing Totally Stable to the wrong side of the front, behind the area to be double needle sculptured.

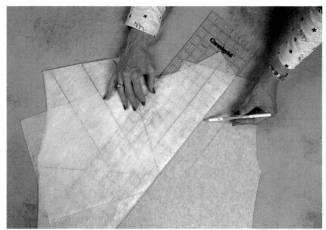

3. To draw sculpture design lines on the fabric front:
a) Lay the fleece front right side up.
b) Lay the traced pattern front with drawn design lines on top of the fleece front.
c) Lay a clear ruler on top of the pattern piece with the long edge exactly along a drawn design line.
d) Fold the pattern piece back over the ruler to expose the fleece. Use a Chacopel pencil or fabric marker to draw the design line on the fleece.
e) Repeat until all sculpture design lines are transferred to the fleece front.

4. Sculpture stitch on the drawn lines. Refer to your test sample for your stitch choice and machine adjustments.

5. For additional emphasis, sculpture stitch a second row, one presser foot width away from and inside the outer two V's. *Caution*: If you are using different colored threads in each needle, pay close attention to the direction you stitch the second rows. Depending on the direction sewn, you can duplicate or mirror image the color scheme.

6. When finished sculpture stitching, remove the stabilizer and discard.

7. Finish the garment per the pattern directions.

A Dozen Double Needle Sculpturing Ideas

Double needle sculpturing offers many opportunities for adding designer details to garments and for adding your personal "sewing signature" to your work.

1. Sculpture stitch around collars, cuffs, or pockets.
2. Outline welt pockets with sculpture stitching.
3. Sculpture stitch along both sides of a zipper.
4. Sculpture trim the edge of a hood.
5. When combining a print and solid fleece, choose a decorative stitch that complements the print. Using colors from the print, sculpture stitch on the solid color fleece yoke, sleeve band, or contrast sleeves.
6. Insert different colors of rayon thread in the needles. The colors can be strong contrasts or subtle tonal differences.
7. Do a double row of double needle sculpturing to actually net four lines of sculpture stitches. Choose four colors of rayon thread in a graduated color scheme, creating an ombre effect.
8. Create your own print fabric - for example, a solid color garment with "sculpture striped" sleeves. This is a great way to tie in the zipper and ribbing colors when you can't find them to match your fabric!
9. Sculpture a "yoke" on a plain garment.
10. If the fleece print is appropriate, sculpture stitch on the print, highlighting certain areas.
11. Frame an embroidery motif.
12. Sculpture stitch a tic-tac-toe grid on a plain front pullover. Appliqué or embroider in some or all of the squares.

Echo Stitching

Echo stitching is done with a number of repetitive rows of sculpture stitching used to emphasize an appliqué, embroidery motif, or fleece print. Like the rings that form when you drop a stone in calm water, echo stitching lines are simple rather than intricate and detailed. Choose uncomplicated shapes to echo.

Simple echo stitching accents these blunt edge applique stars (see blunt edge technique, pages 96-97).

Free-Motion Sculpturing. . . Etching & Shadow Stitching

Etching and shadow stitching are sculpture stitching techniques, free-motion style. Depending on your level of expertise in free-motion embroidery, your designs can be as uncomplicated or as intricate as your skills allow. Until now, all sculpturing has been with the feed dogs up. These techniques are done with the feed dogs lowered.

The two garment ideas offered here (Winter Trees and Wolves) are easy introductions to free-motion sculpturing. Included are very simplistic directions for free-motion embroidery, intended as a starting place for sewers who have never tried this type of stitching. Seasoned free-motion embroiderers will be off and stitching while the rest of us are still testing and experimenting. For both the novice and the veteran, free-motion stitching on fleece is a creative new avenue to pursue.

Since this sculpturing is done with the feed dogs down, the approach is a little different than the sculpturing you've done so far. Instead of stabilizing with Totally Stable, you adhere the fleece to hooped tear-away stabilizer.

Super Easy Etching:
Winter Trees

I got this idea while looking through an expensive sportswear catalog. I saw numerous fleece and Berber pullovers with simple motifs stitched across the chest or as an accent on a shoulder. As I studied the effect, I saw it was just another way of sculpturing!

The Winter Trees motif is the easiest place to start because it's hard to do it wrong. In nature, branches aren't symmetrical and twigs go every which way.

Do a test sample first! Before etching on the actual garment, follow the stabilizing and stitching directions below and practice on a test sample until you are comfortable with the technique and like your stitches.

You Will Need

→ Sculpturing supplies listed on pages 17-19
→ Wooden hoop 3" to 4" larger than your motif (a 10" hoop works well for the trees)
→ 2 yards medium weight tear-away stabilizer

Construction

1. Cut out the garment pieces.
2. When deciding on the placement of the trees, take into account any garment construction details that may interfere with the trees (trimmed neckline, collar rollback, seamlines, topstitching, etc.). Mark with pins or a fabric marker the area where the trees are to be stitched.
3. Using the Winter Trees template on page 30, trace the trees on Solvy (water-soluble stabilizer) using a fabric marker or a permanent pen.

4. Lightly spray KK2000 on the wrong side of the traced Solvy and adhere to the fleece garment piece where the trees are to be stitched.
5. Hoop a piece of medium weight tear-away stabilizer, making it as taut as possible. (Since it is a tear-away stabilizer, you can only make it so taut or it tears away. A lightweight stabilizer won't provide enough tautness and heavyweight stabilizer will distort the stitches when removing. A firm medium weight is the best choice.)

6. Lightly spray KK2000 on the hooped tear-away stabilizer and adhere the fleece, centering the Solvy design.
7. Set your machine as follows:
a) Lower the feed dogs.
b) Set for 2.5mm zigzag width (the stitch length doesn't matter because the feed dogs are lowered and you are in control).
c) If your machine is in a sewing table, lower it to the flatbed position. If you are sewing on a regular table, attach the sewing machine table or extension plate that came with your machine so you have the largest flat sewing surface possible.
d) Thread an embroidery needle with rayon thread. Loosen the needle tension so the stitches pull slightly to the underside. Use regular or lightweight bobbin thread in the bobbin.
e) Slip the hoop with adhered fleece under the needle.
f) You may attach a darning presser foot, free-motion embroidery presser foot, or stitch using no presser foot at all.
g) Lower the presser foot. (If you are stitching with no presser foot, you must remember to do this to engage the thread tension discs. Since there is no presser foot for reference, it's easy to forget to lower the presser foot that isn't there. The result is a rat's nest.)

If this is your first experience with free-motion sewing:

a) Stay relaxed - you don't need a death grip on the hoop (it's easy to get stiff and tense).

b) Sewing this way may be uncomfortable at first, since you don't have the movement of the feed dogs to depend on.

c) Sew at a medium to medium-fast speed and move the hoop in a smooth, even, side-to-side motion. The medium to medium-fast speed keeps the stitches from getting too long. The sideways motion keeps stitches laying neatly on top of each other.

8. With your elbows resting on the table and hands comfortably placed at the sides of the hoop (east and west position), stitch the trees. Stitch a few rows of the center trunk as a base for the branches. Use the main branches as guidelines for the angle of stitching. Fill in as much or as little as you like. Use the outer broken lines as guides for where to stop stitching to maintain the outer shape of the tree. Stitch over the center trunk again to strengthen its dominance. End by stitching the ground shadow at the base of the tree.

d) If you don't like the way a stitched line looks, change your angle or movement until you have a look you like. (That's why you need to do a test sample first.)

Winter Trees is a good first project since tree branches aren't supposed to be symmetrical. If there are gaps or misses, it's easy to go back and fill in or correct as necessary.

9. Remove as much Solvy as possible. Excess Solvy can be rinsed away with warm water. Since KK2000 dissipates on its own, it is recommended that the Solvy not be rinsed away for a couple days. Refer to the KK2000 information on page 14.

10. Remove the tear-away stabilizer from the underside and discard.

11. Finish constructing the garment according to the pattern directions.

Winter Trees Template

Enlarge or reduce to fit your garment

Fleece Appliqué and Shadow Stitching: Wolves

This is a fun idea to use on a garment that combines a print and a solid fleece. Choose a print that offers an appropriate motif (wolf face, tree, geometric design, snowflake) to use for a fleece appliqué. You'll call subtle attention to the appliqué by shadow stitching (transferring outlines of the motif to the solid fleece), "echoing" the appliqué. You can use a shadow stitched motif alone or in multiples. You can trace the motif and enlarge or reduce the size for added interest. For the most pleasant visual effect, when stitching multiple motifs overlap them a little so the overall embellishment flows and has continuity.

This idea works best on garments with separate yokes or blocked sections suitable for combining a print with a coordinate solid fleece. The fleece appliqué and accent shadow stitching are done in the solid fleece areas.

I happened to use a wolf print, but the procedure is the same whether it's snowflakes, leaves, or whatever.

You'll need the wooden hoop and tear-away stabilizer listed for Winter Trees.

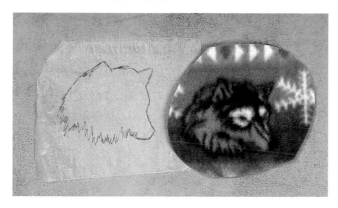

Test Sample

1. Overlay the printed fleece with a piece of Solvy and trace a motif with a permanent felt tip pen. Look at the dominant lines of the motif and decide which lines are appropriate to shadow stitch. Avoid lots of detail (unless you are an experienced free-motion stitcher). This first tracing will be used as the test.

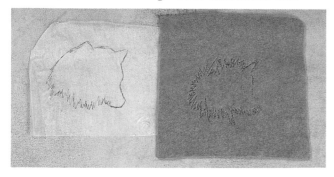

2. Following the directions for Winter Trees, adhere traced Solvy to the solid fleece and adhere fleece to the hooped stabilizer. Then free-motion shadow stitch the traced design. Remove the Solvy and critique the "test" design. Redraw and change lines as needed to get the look you want.

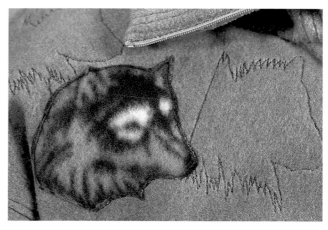

Example: When I traced and stitched the wolf profile exactly the same as the appliqué, the tuft at the back of his neck looked great in the print and on the appliqué, but looked misshapen when shadow stitched. I redrew the profile, eliminating the back neck fur and liked it much better.

The Real Thing

1. Refer to the directions for Winter Trees to decide on the placement of appliqués and shadow stitched motifs. Experiment with different combinations. A nice arrangement is one fleece appliqué with two or three shadow stitched motifs echoing the design. Remember to overlap or butt the designs.

Examples of other ways to use shadow stitching.

2. For the blunt edge fleece appliqué (refer to pages 96-97):

a) From printed fleece, choose a motif for appliqué and shadow stitching. Use sharp scissors that leave a crisp blunt edge to cut out one or more appliqués.

b) Lightly spray KK2000 on the wrong side of the fleece appliqué.

c) Adhere the fleece appliqué in place.

d) Edgestitch in place, using a medium length straight stitch. (There is no need to stabilize the fleece garment when doing a straight stitch appliqué. If the appliqué would look prettier with the traditional satin stitch appliqué edge finish, you will first need to stabilize the garment area with Totally Stable before satin stitching the appliqué.)

3. For each shadow stitch motif:

a) Lightly spray KK2000 on the wrong side of each traced Solvy and adhere the motifs to the garment, underlapping or overlapping as desired.

b) Lightly spray KK2000 on tautly hooped tear-away stabilizer and adhere the fleece.

c) Shadow stitch and remove from the hoop.

d) Remove the excess tear-away stabilizer and discard.

e) Remove as much Solvy as possible.

4. Finish constructing the garment per the pattern directions.

Transferring Designs
or How Do I Get There from Here?

Don't skip this section because you've read about it in *Adventures With Polarfleece*. New products have come into the marketplace that offer easier methods of transferring sculpturing designs to your fleece.

Meandering and gridded designs are easy to sculpture. But what if you want a rose? Or leaves and vines? How do you get the design on the fleece so you can see where to stitch?

Transferring Small Motifs

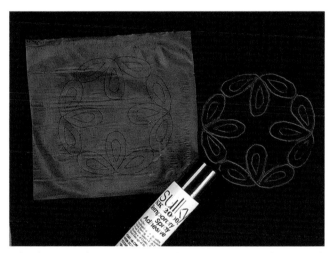

The flower circle motif is featured as a template in the cutwork chapter. Works great for sculpturing too!

1. Stabilize the fleece with Totally Stable.
2. Cut a piece of Solvy a little larger than the motif you want to sculpture.
3. Using a fabric marker or permanent pen, trace the motif.
4. Lightly spray KK2000 on the wrong side of the traced Solvy and adhere to the fleece.
5. Sculpture satin stitch the design.
6. Remove the Solvy.
7. Remove the Totally Stable.

Nancy's Hint

If using a permanent ink pen, I like to choose a color that is compatible with the thread color that will be over it. That way, if the Solvy stabilizer doesn't completely rinse out the first time, any remaining ink lines will blend in with the stitching.

Transferring Large Designs

If a motif is over-sized, tracing and adhering Solvy will be awkward. Using Totally Stable is a much easier way to go. Since Totally Stable is necessary to stabilize the fleece before sculpturing, you simply trace the over-size motif on the Totally Stable *before* adhering it to the fleece.

Be aware: The finished sculpted design will be a reverse of the traced design. If the motif is a one-way design with a right and wrong direction, mirror image it before tracing it on the Totally Stable.

Complete directions and the scroll template for this jacket are found in Adventures With Polarfleece.

1. Trace the design on the papery side of the Totally Stable, mirror imaging if necessary.

2. Press Totally Stable on the wrong side of the garment, placing the design in the desired position.

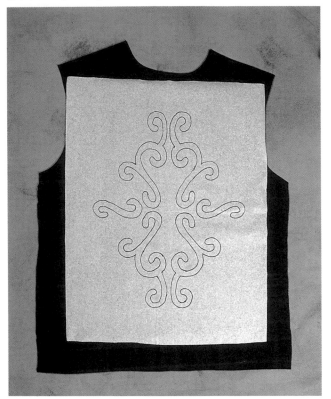

3. To transfer the design to the right side of the garment for sculpture stitching, straight stitch the entire motif from the wrong side of the garment. For better visibility, use a bobbin thread color that will show on the right side (slightly darker or lighter than the fleece color). Don't worry, the sculpture stitching will cover this straight stitch.

4. From the right side of the garment, stitch the sculpturing lines, using the just-stitched bobbin thread as a guideline.

5. If the design is large, you will probably need to roll up the edge of the garment for easy maneuvering. With all the handling, the Totally Stable may separate from the fleece. If this happens, simply press to re-adhere as necessary.

Note: The complete jacket directions and scroll template for sculpturing can be found in *Adventures With Polarfleece*.

Cover Stitch Creations on Polarfleece

This clever use of the wrong side of the cover stitch for texturizing fleece is from Jeanine Twigg. Jeanine is the industry snap expert, founder of The Snap Source, author of *It's a Snap*, and lover of fleece.

Using a cover stitch serger to texture fleece opens up a whole area of serger embellishment. Typically, the cover stitch is used for hemming clothing. The two straight stitching lines are on the right side of the fabric and the lacy zigzag of the looper is on the wrong side. Not on fleece!

The lacy zigzag compresses the fleece, forms a groove, and gives texture and depth to a solid color fleece.

The garment shown was textured with basic black serger thread using the narrow cover stitch.

1. Set your serger for the narrow cover stitch, following the instructions in your serger manual.

2. Thread the two needles and the lower looper, using all the same weight of thread.

3. Cut a generous piece of fleece the length of the project to be textured.

4. Test the cover stitch on scrap fleece. Adjust the tension on the serger to achieve the correct thread balance. When using the cover stitch on fleece, it may be necessary to turn your differential feed to a negative setting (.5 to .7) in order to achieve a smooth textured surface.

5. The cover stitch serging design can be freeform or "pre-mapped." To pre-map your design, use a Chacopel pencil to draw lines and curves on the wrong side of the fleece before stitching.

6. With the *wrong* side of the fleece facing up, cover stitch the fleece on the drawn lines. The wrong side of the fleece will show two straight stitching lines. The right side will be grooved and textured from the zigzag of the looper thread.

7. Using the textured fabric you just created, cut out the garment and sew according to the pattern directions.

Jeanine's Hint

Try not to stitch where snaps will be attached to the fleece. This will allow the snaps to accent the fleece and not overlap the stitching lines. Mark the appropriate snap placement first, and cover stitch the design second.

Be sure to check your serger manual to determine if your serger has the cover stitch capability. Most cover stitch sergers can produce a narrow or wide stitch with two or three needles. Any cover stitch method can be used to texturize fleece, depending on the look you are trying to achieve - narrow or wide stitch, two or three needles. Experiment on scrap pieces of identical fleece before working on the fabric you'll be using to create the project. Have fun - it will look fantastic!

Chapter 3

PINTUCKING – PLAYING WITH DOUBLE NEEDLES

Pintucks are raised welts or tucks of fabric that naturally form between the stitching lines of double needles. Previously a mainstay of heirloom sewing, pintucks have now found their way into everyday sewing - even sewing with fleece.

Pintucks on fleece offer a wide range of applications, from practical to embellishment. Pintucks create classy hem finishes, add interest to a plain collar, and provide depth and interest by texturing plain fleece. You can highlight an embroidery motif or appliqué by framing it with multiple rows of pintucks. Or create borders on hems and sleeves. Or enhance a print. And my favorite - you can use pintucks to make matching "polar ribbing." The possibilities are endless.

Annetta Farr of Spokane, Washington, created this show-stopper using a 3.0 double needle and her quilt bar. Polyester panne velour piping adds elegant contrast with no danger of color transfer.

Marj Ostermiller, a free-lance sewing instructor from Billings, Montana, used 4.0 needles to add these sophisticated design lines to her vests.

Getting Started

Double Needles

Just like regular needles, double needles come in a variety of sizes and types. They also come in a variety of widths (space between the needles).

Choose the needle *size* appropriate for your fleece weight (the same size you would choose for a regular needle).

Choose the needle *type* appropriate for the thread and/or fabric choice.

Choose the needle *width* to match your pintuck presser foot and the desired finished effect you want.

Double Needle Size: Just like regular needles, choose the needle *size* to complement the fabric *weight*. The smaller the number, the finer or smaller the needle. The larger the number, the larger and stronger the needle shaft. Since most fleeces that will be pintucked will be in the mid-weight range, you will most often choose a size 80/12 or 90/14 needle.

Double Needle Type: The *type* of needle is determined by the fabric and thread you're using. Since fleece is a knit fabric, you want a regular universal or stretch (ball) point double needle when pintucking with regular thread.

If you pintuck with rayon thread, use an embroidery needle. (An embroidery double needle has a universal point but offers a larger eye and deeper groove to better accommodate the larger dimension of rayon thread.)

If you pintuck with metallic thread, use a metallic or embroidery double needle. (Again, the larger eye and deeper groove configuration allow the rougher metallic thread to flow more smoothly with less shredding or thread breakage. For best results with metallic thread, use a size 90.)

If there is no specification on the needle package as to type, it is a standard universal needle.

Double Needle Width: There is a third and very important number on a double needle package. This is expressed as a decimal number such as 1.6, 2.0, 2.5, 3.0, 4.0, 6.0, or 8.0. This number refers to the space between the needles in millimeters. Double needles marked 2.5 have a space of 2½ millimeters between the needles. A 4.0 double needle has a wider space of 4 millimeters between the needles. The narrower the width between the needles, the smaller and more delicate the resulting pintuck. The wider the space between the needle, the coarser and bolder the pintuck. Choose the double needle width according to the weight of the fabric, the desired welt appearance, and the capabilities of your machine. Experimentation

will help you determine what you want. When sewing pintucks on fleece, the most frequently used double needles are 3.0 and 4.0.

Nancy's Caution

If considering using wider width double needles, check the zigzag width capabilities of your machine. The maximum zigzag width corresponds with the width of the needle opening on your stitch plate as well as the needle opening on your presser feet. The maximum width between needles should be .5mm less than your machine's maximum zigzag width capability. Narrower needles should not present any problems. Older machines may not be able to use wider than a 3.0 double needle. If you are concerned, hand walk the first few stitches to make sure there is no unwanted contact. If you hear a metallic click, go to a narrower needle. Do not use a 6.0 or wider double needle unless you have a newer machine with wide zigzag capabilities. Refer to your machine manual.

Presser Feet

Presser Foot Choice: If you will be sewing single or random pintucks, you simply need an appliqué or satin stitch presser foot. This foot has a cutout groove on the underside that allows the bulk of the welt to pass smoothly under the presser foot. A regular presser foot with the flat underside would both flatten the welt and balk at letting the welt feed underneath.

If you will be sewing side-by-side pintucks, choose a pintuck presser foot according to the width of the double needle you are using. The grooves on the underside of the presser foot should fit one-on-one to the welt created by the double needle. A 3.0 double needle makes grooves that exactly fit a five-groove presser foot, 4.0 double needle grooves fit a three-groove presser foot. For precise, accurate, evenly spaced pintucks, choose the correct foot for your double needle spacing.

Nancy's Recommendation

I find the most versatile combination is using the 3.0 double needle teamed with the five-groove presser foot. This works on all ages of machines and provides a nice, medium welt on lighter weight through medium/heavy-weight fleeces. Since most often the fleece choice will be mid-weight, the 3.0 needle is perfect.

Stitch Choice

For most pintucking purposes in this chapter, you will use a straight stitch with a longer 3mm to 4mm stitch length. However, don't overlook the creative possibilities that a zigzag, multiple zigzag, serpentine, and other non-satin decorative stitches offer.

When pintucking using a decorative rather than straight stitch, use an appliqué presser foot.

Safety check: As a double check, it's always smart to hand rotate for a few stitches to make sure you did the math correctly and that the needles clear your presser foot and stitch plate. Better safe than sorry!

Double Needle Chart

Nancy's Caution

When choosing one of these decorative stitches, your machine doesn't know you inserted a double needle! To determine the widest possible zigzag width without break-ing a needle, you will need to do a little math. Add .5mm to the needle separation (3.0 or 4.0) and subtract this number from the maximum stitch width available on your machine. (The 3.0 or 4.0 is the actual space between the needles while the .5mm accounts for the actual needle size.) This will give you the widest stitch width you can choose. Consult your machine manual for maximum stitch width capability.

Example: Widest Machine Zigzag	MINUS Needle Separation	PLUS .5mm	EQUALS Max. Width of Decorative Stitch
5mm	(3.0	+ .5)	1.5mm
5mm	(4.0	+ .5)	.5mm
5mm	(6.0	+ .5)	n/a
9mm	(3.0	+ .5)	5.5mm
9mm	(4.0	+ .5)	4.5mm
9mm	(6.0	+ .5)	2.5mm

Since there is a large range of machine width capabili-ties and double needle choices, you have to do the math for your machine and needle choice.

This   Not this

Non-satin stitch   Satin stitch

Nancy's Hint

If you are lucky enough to own a newer computerized machine, engage the double needle function and program in your double needle width. The machine will automatically engage this safety feature and not allow you to choose a too-wide stitch width.

Thread Choice

You can use high quality long staple polyester regular sewing thread in the needles and in the bobbin. You can also use rayon or metallic thread in the needles if desired. Test to see if the sheen of the rayon or the sparkle of the metallic will show. Depending on the loft of the fabric and colors chosen, the decorative thread may not be noticeable.

Regardless of the thread you choose for the needles, use regular thread in the bobbin.

Nancy's Money-Saving Hint

Since the bobbin thread won't be visible, this is a good time to use up all those pesky leftover partial spools of thread. Just make sure they aren't ancient and weakened.

Machine Set-Up

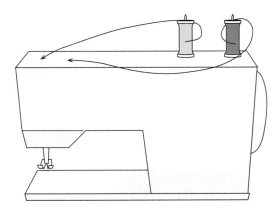

If you have two vertical thread spool holders on the back of your machine, place the left thread so the thread feeds off from the back left side of the spool. Place the right thread so the thread feeds off from the right front side of the spool. This arrangement prevents the thread from tangling.

If you have a horizontal thread spool holder on the back of your machine, your machine should have available a vertical spool holder attachment for the second spool.

If you only have one vertical thread spool holder, place a filled bobbin on the bottom of the spool holder, topping it with your spool of thread. Arrange the bobbin and 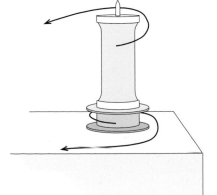 the spool of thread so they rotate in opposite directions as the thread is being pulled off. This arrangement helps prevent thread tangling.

When threading your machine for double needle stitching, separate the threads every time you have the opportunity. Place one thread on the left side of the tension disc and the other thread on the right side of the tension disc. If you have two thread guides going into the needle, use one thread in each guide. If you only have one thread guide, just before you thread the needles you may find that your machine sews nicer if one thread is in the guide and the other thread bypasses the guide. Your test sewing will show you which is the best way.

Nancy's Hint

If you will be sewing lots of pintucks, save time by winding five or six bobbins before you begin. This saves stopping and winding bobbins in the middle of your sewing.

Test Sample

Whether you are making polar ribbing, framing an appliqué, accenting a print, or adding texture to plain fleece, it's important for you to sew a test sample to achieve the look you want.

Beginning with your machine's normal needle tension setting and using a longer stitch length (3mm to 4mm), sew a pintuck row to see how it looks. If you want a more pronounced welt, tighten the upper tension a little and sew a second row to check. If you want a flatter, less pronounced welt, loosen the upper tension. Sew a row and check.

Do this test sewing on both the straight of grain and on the crossgrain. Alter your stitch length or tension if necessary so the pintucks look the same when sewn on both grainlines. (Usually the settings are the same, but this simple quick check could save potential disappointment later.)

Pintucks on the lengthwise grain easily maintain straight crisp lines. Depending on the degree of crossgrain stretch, multiple rows of pintucks on the crossgrain may wave. Sew a test piece to see. Lengthen the stitch and lighten the presser foot pressure to reduce rippling, if necessary.

Note: Some fleeces may have a nap that changes the appearance of pintucks sewn in opposite directions. Your test sample will tell you. If nap changes are obvious, sew all pintucks in the same direction (with the nap).

Pintuck Spacing

Depending on the look you want and the intended purpose of the pintucks, you can space the grooves right alongside each other or inches apart. To prevent any possible twisting or distortion, reverse the direction of sewing pintuck rows every couple inches (or every so many rows) if there is no nap difference.

For evenly spaced pintuck grooves, use the appropriate presser foot for the double needle chosen. Using the most popular choices for fleece - the 3.0 and the 4.0 - here are some pintuck spacing options:

Large, evenly spaced pintuck designs are easy when using your machine's quilt bar.

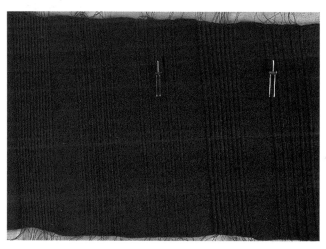

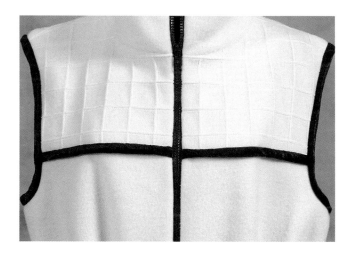

Textured Stripes and Lattice Look: Sew the first pintuck row. Space the next pintuck rows as desired. For an easy way to space pintucks, attach a quilt bar, edge guide, or spacer bar to your machine. Depending on your machine, these handy tools attach either to the presser foot or the presser foot shank. Simply adjust for the spacing you want between rows and sew the remaining pintuck rows. (This is much easier than drawing all the lines in place.) This technique is especially nice to use when creating an all-over design.

Side-by-Side (a tight, grooved look): Sew one pintuck row. Lift the presser foot and slide the just-sewn pintuck over one groove (to be under the groove adjacent to the center groove). Sew the second pintuck row. The presser foot groove guides and controls the first pintuck, aligning it perfectly alongside the second pintucked row. Repeat the process, sewing pintuck rows side-by-side. Quick and easy.

Ribbed Look: Sew one pintuck row. Lift the presser foot and align the just-sewn pintuck under the outermost groove (skipping one groove) and sew the next row. Continue sewing, skipping one groove.

Spaced Ribbed Look: Same as the ribbed look except the spacing is wider, aligning the outer edge of the presser foot against each welt as you sew the next row.

Which Comes First - Pintucking or Cutting?

The golden rule of sewing says that you should pintuck the fabric first and cut out the garment pieces second. This is because pintucks take up a little bit of fabric in every welt and alter the width of the fabric. In theory that's true. But because fleece garments are generally more loosely fitted, some pintucking rules can be broken.

If your garment offers a looser fit and the pintucks will be used in moderation, you can cut out the garment pieces first and pintuck second. Since there won't be rows and rows of pintucks, the change to the fabric width will be minimal and not affect the overall looser fit of the garment. (Examples: cascading pintucks, framing a design, outlining a print.)

If you are sewing rows and rows of pintucks, pintuck the fabric first and cut out the garment pieces second. Sewing so many rows of pintucks will alter the fabric width enough to make a difference. (Examples: polar ribbing, pintucking in stripes or grids to create a textured fabric.)

Securing Pintucked Ends

If the ends of the pintucked fabric will be incorporated into a seamline, simply backtack or stitch in place a few stitches when beginning and ending a pintuck row (garment pieces cut first, pintucked second).

If the garment pieces will be cut from pintucked fabric, use a shorter stitch length when sewing the garment seams. Doublestitch or topstitch if appropriate, to further secure the thread ends.

If pintucks are used as a free-standing design where backtacking or stitching in place would be visible, pull the needle threads to the underside and tie in a knot to secure. (Example: framing, outlining a print.)

Pivoting Corners

Since two needles are penetrating the fabric, a simple "sink the needle and turn" pivot won't work. To "get around the corner" you'll need to take a couple of steps.

To pivot a pintucked corner:

1. Sew up to within a stitch or two of the exact corner.
2. Stop with the needles down in the fabric.
3. Raise the presser foot and pivot the fabric until the double needles begin to slightly twist.
4. Lower the presser foot.
5. Take one stitch, again stopping with the needles down in the fabric.
6. Raise the presser foot and again pivot the fabric until the double needles begin to slightly twist.
7. Lower the presser foot.

8. Take one stitch, stopping with the needles down in the fabric.
9. Pivot as above if necessary, and continue sewing. This results in an angled rather than sharp corner.

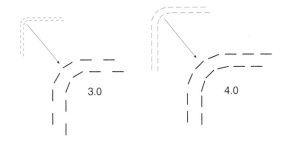

Note: The wider the double needle, the more "stop-and-pivot" single angled stitches are needed to get around the corner. Narrow double needles can frequently pivot with only one angled corner stitch. Wider needles need two or three pivot steps to make the turn. The wider the needle and/or the stiffer the fabric, the more stitches you'll need to get around the corner.

Caution: Use a gentle touch when pivoting and twisting the double needles. If you twist too hard, you may break or bend a needle.

Troubleshooting: If you skipped a stitch at the corner, it's because the machine was not allowed to complete the stitch before pivoting. Make sure the needles have gone completely down to the lowest position in the machine before pivoting. This position allows the needles to catch the bobbin thread and complete the stitch. The machine must be sewing forward and stop needle down. If you back up by hand rotating the wheel, the needles will miss the bobbin thread and skip a stitch.

Now that we've covered all the basics…

Let's play!

Playing With Pintucks

Polar Ribbing: Double Needle Ribbing

I have used double needles to make pintuck ribbing on other knits, but somehow never thought about using this simple technique on fleece. My thanks go to Rosemary Kozdra, a sewing instructor at Malden Mills Retail Store in Lawrence, Mass., for "polar ribbing." When I was giving a seminar at the store, Rosemary showed me how well this idea worked on her gorgeous jackets.

So much of the appeal of expensive polar ready-made garments is found in the coordinating details like matching ribbing. With double needles and a couple extra spools of thread, you can easily make your own matching polar ribbing! Choose fleece rather than Berber or plush for this technique.

Polar ribbing is perfect to use for cuffs, bottom bands, stand-up collars, and even traditional collars! Since polar ribbing is made from self fabric, it won't have as much stretch or recovery as real ribbing. If you want to use it as the neck trim on a pullover, choose a pattern that allows for self-fabric neck trim. Before constructing, hold the polar ribbing around your head and neck to check for desired fit and feel.

Polar ribbing takes on a variety of appearances.

Option #1

Option #2

Option #3

Option #4

Mix 'n Match Fleece Ideas For the Look You Prefer

Option #1: Make the garment from one fabric, solid or print, making self-fabric polar ribbing.

Option #2: Make the garment body from solid color fleece and the sleeves from print fleece. Use the print fleece to make coordinating polar ribbing. Appliqué a chest band if the print is appropriate.

Option #3: Make the garment body from print fleece and the sleeves from a coordinate solid. Use the solid fleece to make polar ribbing.

Option #4: If the print is appropriate, cut out a band of print fleece and blunt edge appliqué it across the solid color garment front (see pages 96-97.) Use the print fleece to make coordinating polar ribbing.

Figuring Yardage for Polar Ribbing

Pintucking the fleece will turn it into a ribbed-looking fabric but will not give the fleece any more stretch than it had to start with. Before making polar ribbing, make sure your fleece has enough crossgrain stretch to work as a band, collar, or cuffs.

Polar ribbing will be made from 7" cuts of fleece cut on the crossgrain. If the print is such that you want to center a motif in the ribbing, then compute yardage by figuring one print repeat for each cut. (If the repeat is less than 7", consider it to be an overall print or buy extra to center the design on bands and collar.)

To make polar ribbing for a bottom band, cuffs, and collar, you'll need 5/8 yard of solid color or an overall print or three repeats (which will include enough for a chest appliqué).

How to Make Polar Ribbing

1. Wind five or six bobbins with regular thread.

2. Insert a 3.0 double needle.

3. Using two spools of thread, thread the machine and both needles.

4. Attach a five-groove pintuck presser foot to your machine.

5. Cut a test scrap of fleece, 7" x 10" or so, with the

greater stretch in the length (crossgrain).

6. Test sew a pintuck row using regular tension and a 3mm to 3.5mm stitch length to see if you like the resulting welt. Tighten the needle tension for a more pronounced welt or loosen it for a flatter welt.

7. Experiment with the spacing of pintucks for the ribbing look you prefer. Choose either *side-by-side* (spacing pintucks in every groove for a tight ribbed look), *ribbed* (spacing pintuck rows every other groove for a 1 x 2 ribbing look), or *spaced ribbed* (spacing rows a presser foot width apart for a coarser wide ribbed look). *Caution*: Side-by-side restricts the stretch (refer to pintuck spacing information on page 40).

8. Cut 7" x 60" strips of fleece for polar ribbing (with the greater stretch going in the length). The 7" width allows room to straighten the edges after pintucking.

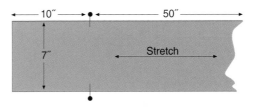

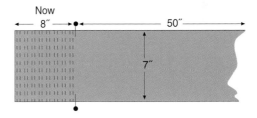

9. To estimate the quantity of fleece you need to pintuck, use the first 10" of a fleece strip as a "rib gauge."

a) Use pins or a fabric marker to mark 10" from one selvage end.

b) Using your chosen needle tension and rib spacing, begin 1/2" from the end of the fleece strip and pintuck the marked 10" section. To avoid distortion, after sewing an inch or two of pintuck rows, reverse the fabric and sew from the other direction. Sew pintuck rows to fill the rib gauge section, continuing to reverse direction every couple inches. (If the fleece shows a nap, stitch all the rows in the same direction.)

c) Measure the rib gauge section and compare the measurements before and after pintucking. If the original 10" length is now 8" (having been drawn up by the welts of the pintucks), 20% of the original length was lost to pintucking. Use this information to figure approximately how much fleece length you will need to pintuck for cuffs, lower band, and collar. (This is nicer than pintucking two more feet than you actually need!)

d) If there is a definite design in your fleece print, pintuck a little extra to allow for a flattering motif placement on the collar and to space as desired on the cuffs and lower band.

Caution: If you will be using part of the fleece print as an appliqué across the chest, don't get carried away in the pintucking process and pintuck everything! Leave enough unribbed print for the chest band appliqué.

Polar Ribbing No-Fail Stand-Up Collar

Betty Acheson used the quick and easy blunt edge applique technique for the snowflake motif across the chest. She then made self-fabric polar ribbing for the perfect finishing touch.

If your pattern features a zipper-through-the-collar design, you'll like this simple alteration that gives you no-fail matched collar edges every time.

When a stand-up collar calls for the zipper to end at squared corners, if anything is the slightest bit off, the mismatch is frustratingly obvious. Rather than rip out and re-do, perform this simple pattern alteration to insure success the first time.

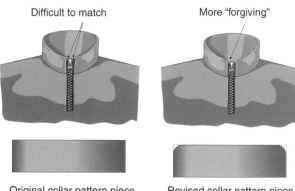

Difficult to match

More "forgiving"

Original collar pattern piece

Revised collar pattern piece

1. Before beginning construction, slightly round off the upper collar points. Mark dots on the outer and side edges 1" from the corners and draw a curve.

2. When inserting the zipper, place the upper end of the zipper 1/2" below the curved top edge.

If this step makes your zipper too long, refer to the no-bulk zipper shortening technique in the No-Hassle Zippers chapter in *Adventures With Polarfleece*.

Nancy's Comment

Since tearing out is not my idea of fun, I refer to this technique as my "cut potential losses early" insurance. With the rounded corners and offset zipper, if the upper edges don't quite match, no one is any the wiser! I use this simple pattern alteration on almost all my collars, even those not made from polar ribbing.

Polar Ribbing Cuffs & Bottom Band

Since polar ribbing doesn't have as much stretch or recovery as real ribbing, adjust the length of ribbing used for the cuffs and bottom band as follows:

Cuffs: Fold the polar ribbing in half lengthwise and cut it long enough to comfortably slip your hand through. Add 1/2" for the seam allowance. If using a printed fleece, plan for centering a motif if applicable.

Bottom Band: Fold the polar ribbing in half lengthwise and hold it around your hip area for a comfortable fit. Add 1/2" for the seam allowance. If using a print fleece, plan for centering a motif at the center front if applicable.

When sewing the cuffs and band into a circle, use a conventional sewing machine and finger press the seam allowance open. (A serger seam would be too bulky.)

To compensate for less stretch in polar ribbing, run two rows of gathering stitches along the lower edge of the sleeve and the lower edge of the garment. Gather the garment to be slightly larger than the ribbing cuff or bottom band dimension. Sew the ribbing to the garment using a 3.5mm or 4mm stitch length. Remove the gathering stitches.

Ribbed Insets

Another great accent for sportswear is the addition of an accent band across the garment chest or across a sleeve. Knitters frequently use this look in ski sweaters. Resorts and boutiques incorporate this idea in expensive sportswear.

Ribbed insets are sewn the same as polar ribbing. The only difference is that they are inset as panels instead of applied as trim. This is a great way to spice up a solid color garment! It's perfect for pullovers, jackets, and vests, and a great way to use a pretty leftover print scrap that's too small for anything else but too pretty to throw away.

Choose a solid color fleece fabric as the base for your garment and a coordinating print with a suitable design to be used as a 4" to 6" inset. Since the ribbing technique will add a little weight to the print, choose fleeces with comparable weights.

Decide where you want the insets:
a) Across the chest area.
b) Across the upper sleeve (one or both sleeves).
c) Across the lower edge of the sleeve, above the cuffs.

Drafting Your Pattern for Insets
1. Trace the pattern front, back, and sleeves. Label and draw in the straight-of-grain lines.
2. Decide on the placement of the inset and draw the inset lines on the pattern piece. (The example shown is for a 5" inset.)

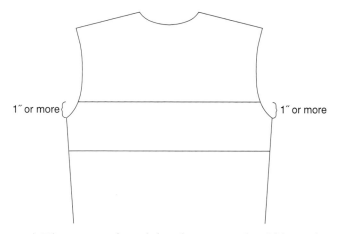

1˝ or more   1˝ or more

a) The upper edge of the chest inset should be at least 1" above the underarm point to eliminate extra bulk that would result from multiple seams in the same area.

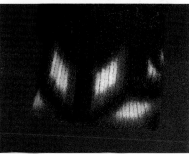

Polar ribbing looks so expensive and is so easy to make!

Here's a great use for a leftover piece of a dynamic print.

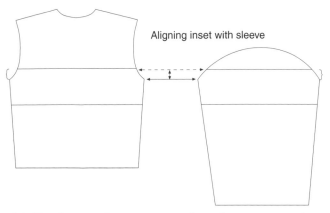

Aligning inset with sleeve

b) To align a chest inset with a sleeve inset, draw placement lines for the chest inset first. Then draw the line for the upper edge of the sleeve inset the same distance above the armscye point as the chest inset.

c) If placing the inset at the lower edge of the sleeve, allow a minimum 2" above the cuff for blouson.

d) The chest band can be on the front only or on both the front and back, as desired.

5. Cut out the fabric, using the just-made polar ribbed print fleece for the insets.

6. Sew the insets to the garment to make a complete front or complete sleeve. Sew with a 3/8" seam allowance. Finger press the seam allowance toward the garment (away from the inset) and topstitch at 1/4" to secure. Use a longer 3.5mm to 4mm stitch length to topstitch.

7. Finish the garment per the pattern directions.

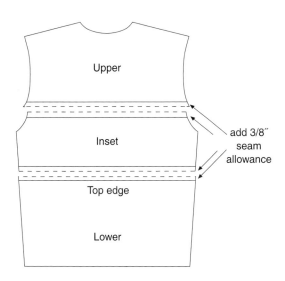

Upper

Inset

add 3/8″ seam allowance

Top edge

Lower

3. Cut the pattern pieces apart (not the fabric yet, only the pattern pieces) on the drawn inset lines and add 3/8" seam allowance to all newly cut edges.

4. Label the newly drafted pattern pieces with all the pertinent information (upper front, lower front, chest inset, upper sleeve, lower sleeve, sleeve inset).

Spice up ordinary garments with a smidgen of ribbed Polarfleece here or a dash of ribbed fleece there.

Double Needle Impressions

Is subtlety more your style? Use double needle impressions to add your personality to your garments. Double needle impressions simply use the raised welts of pintucks to add subtle texture and depth to your sewing. Not so much a knock-their-socks-off-as-you-walk-in-the-door technique, but rather an understated effect that catches their eye as they ask, "How did you do that?"

Nancy's Note

When doing little bits of pintucking, you can cut out your garment first and pintuck second. Since fleece garments are looser in fit and since little bits of pintucking won't greatly affect the fit, it is easier to do the pintuck accents on the cutout garment pieces. If you are doing lots and lots of rows of pintucking - enough to actually alter the dimension of your fabric (like in polar ribbing) - then it's necessary to pintuck the fabric first and cut out the garment second. Most of the ideas offered here are not enough to alter the dimensions. When necessary, you will be directed to pintuck first and cut second.

Tone-on-Tone Impressions

This technique uses pintuck welts to create a soft, subtle design. Use it to dress up a plain garment, add texture to an appliqué, or texture a block.

For best results, use medium-sized simple shapes. Avoid small details. For the least fabric distortion around the designs, motifs should be 4" or less in width. There are no height restrictions. Some good designs are diamonds, hearts, simple bows, sailboats, cat or dog outlines, and simple flowers like tulips. Seasonal motifs like Christmas trees or shamrocks also work well. Card players can make a four square framework grid and make an impression using the spade, heart, diamond, and club motif (templates are on pages 49-50).

1. Cut out the garment and decide on the placement of the impression. Be sure to allow for neckline trimming, seam allowances, and any construction details that may interfere with the design.
2. Cut a piece of Totally Stable 4" larger than your design on all sides.
3. Trace the outline of your design on the paper side of the Totally Stable.

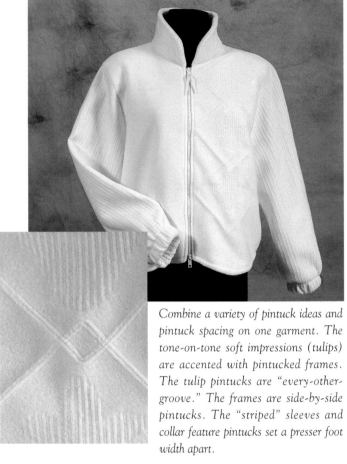

Combine a variety of pintuck ideas and pintuck spacing on one garment. The tone-on-tone soft impressions (tulips) are accented with pintucked frames. The tulip pintucks are "every-other-groove." The frames are side-by-side pintucks. The "striped" sleeves and collar feature pintucks set a presser foot width apart.

4. Cut out and discard the design itself, leaving a "stencil" of the design. (You will pintuck inside the opening of the stencil.)
5. Place the design stencil on the *right* side of your garment. Using a dry iron and lower temperature, lightly press the stencil to adhere. Cover the open area with a press cloth.

Nancy's Caution

Press the Totally Stable stencil with a gentle touch and a cooler iron. This is only a temporary adhesion. If the iron is too hot or if you press too long, the Totally Stable will adhere too tightly and possibly de-fleece your fabric when you remove it.

6. Using a fabric marker, draw a line down the center of your motif, designating where you will begin stitching. (This line will *always* be going up-and-down on the lengthwise straight of grain, so you will *always* pintuck the motif in the direction of least stretch.)

7. Using a 3.0 double needle and a five-groove pintuck presser foot, stitch a test pintuck sample on a scrap of fleece. Sew on the lengthwise grain. Adjust the upper tension as necessary to achieve a moderately raised welt between the double needles (deep welts will distort the fabric too much).

8. Stitch on the drawn line, starting and stopping just inside the Totally Stable stencil, leaving long enough thread tails at both ends to later pull through and tie off on the underside. Do not backtack.

9. To stitch the second row, align the first welt under the outside groove of the presser foot (ribbed look), and stitch the beginning and end just inside the Totally Stable stencil. Continue stitching rows, aligning the previously sewn row in the outermost groove, until the design is filled. Leave long thread tails at the beginning and end of each row.

10. Carefully remove the Totally Stable stencil and discard.

11. Pull all the thread tails to the underside and tie off to secure.

12. If there is slight puckering around the design, steam from the wrong side and finger press to smooth the area. Do not touch the iron to the fleece.

13. Construct the garment per pattern directions.

Nancy's Notes

It's important to align the previously sewn welt under the outside groove. This has the welts spaced every other groove. If you were to sew the welts right next to each other in every groove, it would draw up too much fabric and distort the surrounding fabric. For the most visible pintucks, choose a flatter rather than thick napped fleece and use darker thread in the needles.

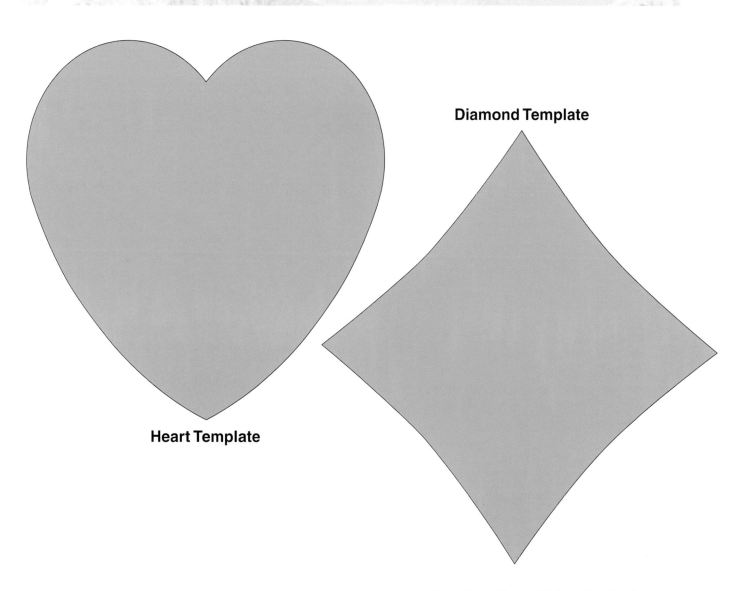

Heart Template

Diamond Template

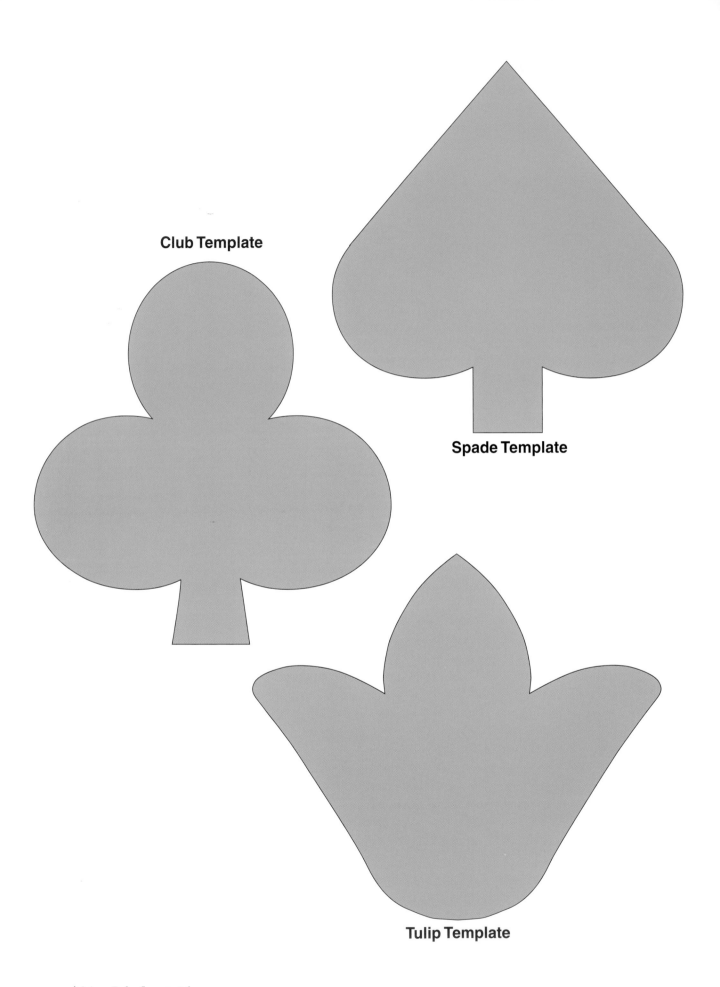

Club Template

Spade Template

Tulip Template

Cascading Pintucks

A feminine touch that adds interest to a solid garment front, a plain sleeve cap, or can be incorporated into a blocked design.

Garment Front

Sew double needle pintucks cascading down from the neckline.

Deep yoke with cowl neck

1. Using a fabric marker, draw a line on the center front on the garment, extending 8" below the neck edge.

2. Using a 3.0 double needle and five-groove pintuck presser foot, sew the center pintuck. Do not backtack at the bottom edge. Leave thread tails long enough to pull through and tie off on the underside when finished pintucking.

3. Sew a row on either side of the center pintuck, using the outside edge of the presser foot as a guide (spaced ribbed look). Stop 1" above the center pintuck. Leave long thread tails.

4. Continue sewing pintuck rows on either side, each time shortening the pintuck length by 1". Add rows until you have the look you want.

5. Pull all the long thread tails through to the underside and tie off to secure.

Nancy's Note

The wide spacing of the pintucks will not greatly alter the garment's dimension or fit. If you want closer-spaced pintucks and plan the width of the cascade to be wider than 4", pintuck first and cut out the garment second. Or if your garment has a closer fit, pintuck first and cut second.

Shoulder Accent

Create a design with cascading pintucks falling from one or both shoulders.

1. With a fabric marker, mark the placement and length of the longest pintuck row.

2. Using a 3.0 double needle and a five-groove pintuck presser foot, stitch from the shoulder to the end of the row. Do not backtack. Leave thread tails long enough to pull through and tie off on the underside when finished pintucking.

3. Sew the next row of pintucking, using the outside edge of the presser foot as a spacing guide. Stop 1" above the end of the first pintuck.

4. Continue sewing pintuck rows, each time shortening the length by 1", until you have the look you want.

5. Pull all the long thread tails through to the underside and tie off to secure.

Sleeve Caps

Sew double needle pintucks cascading down from the sleeve cap.

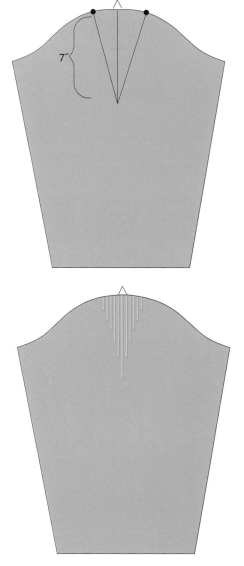

1. Using a fabric marker, mark the center of the sleeve cap and at 2" either side of the center mark.

2. Draw a line on the center of the sleeve, extending 7" from the top of the sleeve cap.

3. Draw a V from the end of the line to the outside marks.

4. Using a 3.0 double needle and a five-groove pintuck presser foot, pintuck on the center line.

5. Pintuck rows on either side of the center row, spacing the welts in every other groove of the presser foot. Stop when you reach the drawn V line. Do not backtack. Leave long thread tails.

6. Pull all the long thread tails through to the underside and tie off to secure.

Blocked Design

In a blocked plain garment front, one or several blocks can feature simple cascading pintucks. The garment front could be color blocked, solid color and print blocked, overlaid with cotton prints for blocking, or texture blocked. For a lovely windowpane effect, topstitch narrow strips of UltraSuede over the blocking lines.

1. Cut a plain front garment pattern apart into blocked sections.

2. Add seam allowances if you will be sewing the sections back together. Leave cut sections as is if you will be butting edges and topping them with a trim strip.

3. Draw a line for the center pintuck.

4. Using a 3.0 double needle and a five-groove pintuck presser foot, pintuck the center welt. Stitch in place at the beginning (the cut edge of the block) and leave long thread tails at the end of the pintuck.

5. Pintuck the rows on either side of the center row, spacing the welts in every other groove of the presser foot. Sew a total of seven to nine pintuck rows. Pull through and tie off thread tails to the underside.

6. Sew the blocks together to form the garment front and finish constructing the garment according to the pattern directions.

Pintucked Plaid or Stripes

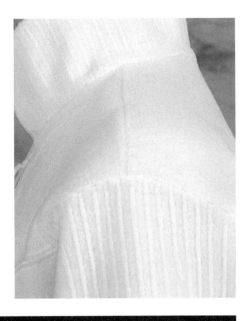

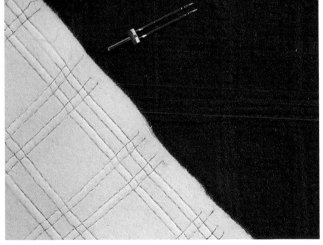

Start with a plain solid colored fleece and pintuck your own textured plaid or stripes! Copy the spacing from a plaid you like or make up one of your own.

With a piece of plain paper, pencil, and ruler, draw lines and experiment with spacing until you have a plaid or stripe you like. Just like in real plaids, line spacing can create an even or uneven plaid.

For quick and easy spacing of the "closer" plaid lines, use the grooves on the underside of the pintuck presser foot and space welts every groove, every other groove, or at the outer edge of the presser foot. For wider line spacing, use your quilt bar, edge guide, or spacer bar. (See textured stripes and lattice look on page 40.)

Sew pintuck plaid lines on the lengthwise and crosswise straight-of-grain lines. If necessary, lengthen the stitch and/or lighten the pressure on the presser foot for less distortion when sewing on the crossgrain.

Nancy's Note

In this instance, since you are sewing quite a few rows of pintucking, you will probably alter the finished dimension of the fabric. For this application, it is best to pintuck the plaid or stripes first and cut out the garment second.

Tic Tac Toe Shirt

Using your favorite plain front pullover sweatshirt-style pattern, reminisce while you re-create this favorite childhood game.

1. Cut out the garment from solid color fleece.

2. Using a fabric marker, draw horizontal and vertical lines for a traditional tic tac toe grid.

Nancy's Hints

#1 *Hold the garment up to your body in front of a mirror and mark with pins for a flattering placement level for the horizontal grid lines.*

#2 *Draw lines to avoid bulky crossing of multiple seamlines.*

Make sure the vertical lines are at least 1" away from the neckline shoulder point. Depending on how large or small you want the center square, these lines can end in the neck edge or at the shoulder line. (Check the pattern to see if the neckline will be trimmed before adding the rib trim finish. Draw in the neck seamline accordingly.)

Make sure the horizontal lines are at least 1" above or below the armscye point.

3. Choose a 4.0 double needle and a three-groove pintuck presser foot (for medium to heavier weight fleece) or a 3.0 double needle and a five-groove pintuck presser foot (for medium to lighter weight fleece). Pintuck three side-by-side rows (using adja-cent pintuck grooves on the presser foot) to form the tic tac toe grid.

4. Using a drinking glass, small bowl, or compass, draw circles for the O's in a couple of the squares.

5. Draw X's in some squares.

6. Again using the double needle and appropriate pintuck presser foot, sew three side-by-side pintucks to form the X's and O's. Since backtacking would probably be visible and undesirable, pull the thread tails to the underside and tie off to secure the beginning and ending stitching.

7. Complete the garment per the pattern directions.

Nancy's Caution

Be careful where you place the circles. Look in the mirror to see if placement is appropriate. It is safer (and more flattering) to let the X's win this game!

Adding Classy Design Lines to a Simple Garment

All you want is a plain and simple walking coat or vest. Solid color. No embellishment or fuss. But being the creative sewer you are, you want just a "little something" that adds your personal signature to the garment. The addition of a few pintuck welts can add classy detail and interest without overpowering the simplicity of the garment.

1. Choose a solid color, medium to heavyweight dense fleece suitable for a jacket.
2. Using a fabric marker, draw design lines on the cutout garment pieces before construction. Be aware of seamlines, pockets, and other construction details that could interfere with the pintucks.

Nancy's Hint

For an easy way to draw straight design lines on the garment, refer to the double needle sculptured pullover in Chapter 2 (page 27).

3. When in doubt as to whether to add another pintuck line...don't. Less is better than more.
4. When drawing lines on a sleeve hem, mark the center of the sleeve. Place interesting corners or angles at the sleeve center.
5. Using a 4.0 double needle and a three-groove pintuck presser foot, sew on the drawn lines. (See instructions for pivoting corners on page 41.)

 Framing

Use two or three rows of side-by-side or ribbed pintucks to frame and add importance to an embroidery motif or appliqué design.

1. After embroidering or appliquéing the design, use a fabric marker and ruler to draw a box (frame) around the design.
2. Using a 3.0 double needle and a five-groove pintuck presser foot and a 3mm to 3.5mm stitch length, pintuck stitch the first line of the frame. Begin on one long side of the box, don't start at a corner. Do not backtack. Leave thread tails long enough to pull through and tie off on the underside.
3. To pintuck the corners, refer to the instructions for pivoting corners on page 41.
4. Alter the stitch length and/or tensions if necessary as you change grainlines.
5. Sew the second row of pintucking, spacing the welt as desired. Sew the second row the same as the first, starting and ending at a different long side of the box.
6. Sew the third row of pintucking, again starting and ending at a different side of the box.
7. Pull all the thread tails through to the underside and tie off to secure.

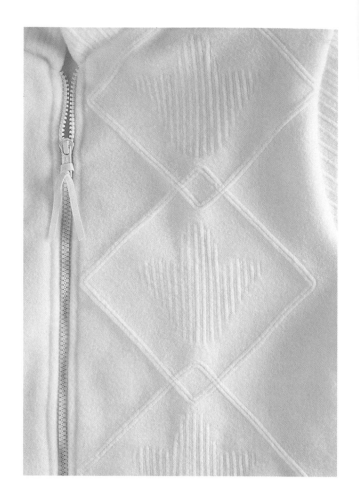

Finishing Touches

→ Instead of plain topstitching for hems, pintuck topstitch the hem! Stitch one row or multiple rows (three to five rows create a nice border effect at the hemline). If your garment has side seam slits, refer to the instructions for pivoting corners on page 41.

→ Instead of topstitching a pocket facing in place, pintuck stitch the facing. Instead of a simple straight stitch line, you will have a lovely welt.

→ Add a pintucked border above the ribbed cuff on an otherwise plain sleeve. Sew three to five pintuck rows, starting at least 2" above the cuff seamline.

→ Would a chest band appliqué or ribbed inset benefit from a touch more accent? Border it with pintucks! After applying the chest band blunt edge appliqué (pages 96-97) or the ribbed chest band inset (pages 45-46), sew three side-by-side or spaced pintucked rows 1" above and below the band.

Nancy's Caution

If you will be pintucking on the crossgrain (the direction with the most stretch), you may need to lengthen the stitch length and/or slightly lighten the pressure of the presser foot to prevent stretching. Sew a pintuck on the crossgrain of scrap fleece to test.

Pintucks With Flair

Crazy Patch Pintuck

Looks complicated, but it's not! Choose a pattern with simple lines and easy fit. Avoid fitted styles with darts, princess lines, or lots of detail. The illustrations here show a simple vest pattern.

1. Pintuck a piece of fabric.
2. Cut it into "crazy patches."
3. Butt the patches together and join!
4. Overlay the butted seams with topstitched narrow strips of UltraSuede, bias trim strips, or decorative braid.

You Will Need

→ Simple plain front vest, jacket, or pullover pattern
→ Medium weight, high quality solid color fleece, yardage per pattern plus 1/2 yard
→ Lining fabric
→ Edgestitch presser foot (optional, but very nice to have)
→ 2" to 3" UltraSuede or 6 yards of 3/8" decorative trim
→ Wash-away double-sided basting tape
→ Five-groove pintuck presser foot and 3.0 double needle OR three-groove pintuck presser foot and 4.0 double needle
→ Decorative thread for topstitching trim (optional)

Being a neat and orderly (translate as "controlled") person, I like to have an exact picture in mind and control every step of the way. I prefer this approach when sewing a crazy patch design because I know where I'm going and what it will look like when I'm finished. The crazy patch layout is first drawn on the garment pattern piece and then cut out from pintucked fabric. Instead of working on a foundation fabric, you butt and join the patches together.

1. Trace a left and right front from a simple vest pattern.
2. With the traced pattern pieces right sides up, draw sections for the crazy patches on both fronts. Keep it simple. Fewer large patches are more dramatic and visually more pleasing than a lot of little patches. Experiment until you have a balance you like. Left

and right fronts do not match - they are complementary to but completely different from each other.

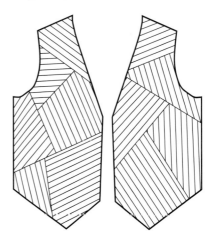

3. In each patch, sketch in the lines for the angle of pintucks.
4. To avoid potential confusion or errors later, number each patch and label as left or right (as when wearing). This is especially helpful if you construct the vest over a number of sewing sessions.
5. Cut out the fleece vest back from plain (untucked) fleece.

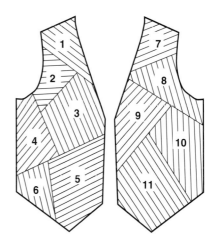

6. Pintuck the remaining fleece, sewing pintucks on the lengthwise straight of grain (direction of least stretch). Sew the first pintuck row. Using a quilt bar, edge guide, or spaced bar, space the remaining pintucks 3/4" from each other.
7. Cut out the crazy patches, using the sketched lines as a guide for the direction of the pintucks.

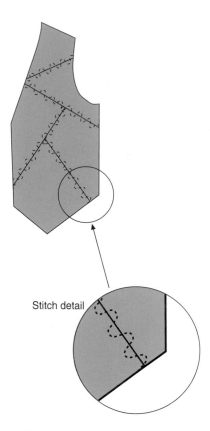

Stitch detail

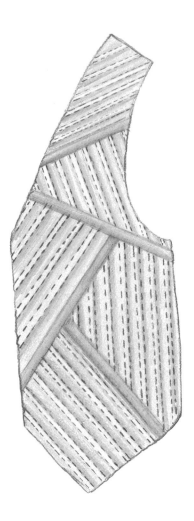

8. Butting the crazy patch edges next to each other, join the pieces to form a complete left and right front.

Nancy's Hints

#1 *For an easy way to join the crazy patches, use an edgestitch presser foot as a guide for centering the seam. Use a wide multiple zigzag or serpentine stitch to join. These are not strong seams. Strength will be added when the seams are topstitched with trim strips.*

#2 *For a stronger pieced front, cut out a complete right and left front from another base fabric such a muslin or lining. Arrange the crazy patch pieces on this base fabric. When the butted edges are sewn together with joining stitches, the base will be incorporated into the stitching.*

9. If using UltraSuede for the trim, cut the suede into 3/8" x 45" strips.
10. Adhere wash-away basting tape to the wrong side of the trim strips.
11. Adhere the trim strips to the vest front, centering the trim over the joined seams. Plan the order of applying the trim strips so the strips overlap and underlap where necessary.

12. Using the 4.0 double needle, topstitch the trim in place. Loosen the needle tension so no welt forms between the stitching lines. Sew the underlapped trim strips first and the overlapped strips last. (*Optional:* Instead of double needle topstitching, edgestitch both edges of the trim in place using a single needle.)

Herringbone Pintucks

Love the look of classic herringbone? Crave the warmth and comfort of fleece? Combine them and get the best of both worlds!

"Herringbone" a vest front, a chest band, a jacket front, or use it to texture block a plain garment.

1. Trace the garment on pattern tracing material.

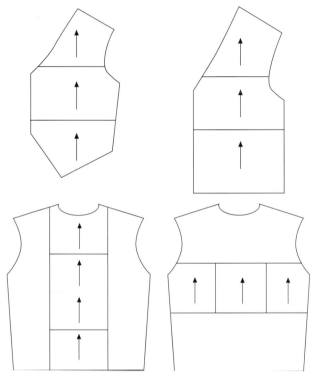

2. Divide the garment into the sections that are to be herringbone-pintucked. (You need a minimum of three divisions or sections to get the herringbone effect.)

3. Draw in straight-of-grain lines in all sections to be herringboned.

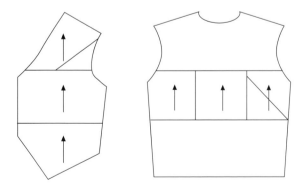

4. In the first or top section, draw a line intersecting the straight-of-grain line at a 45° angle. Make sure the angled line touches the bottom of the section.

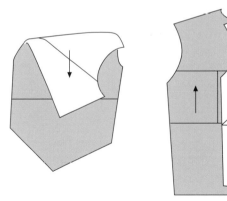

5. Fold over the first section onto the adjacent section, folding on the sectional division or dividing line.

6. Trace the bias line on the second section.

7. Repeat the process, folding the second section onto the third and trace the bias line. Repeat as necessary until all sections have bias lines. It is not necessary for the subsequent lines to touch the horizontal dividing lines. The bias lines simply serve as a guideline for aligning pintucks during the fabric layout.

8. To avoid potential confusion or error in the cutting and sewing process, label all pattern piece sections (upper, middle, lower, right, center, left, etc.). As a further safeguard against problems, also label the top edges of each herringbone section.

9. Cut the herringbone pattern pieces apart and add a 3/8" seam allowance to all newly cut edges.

10. From plain fleece, cut out the garment pieces that will not be pintucked.

11. Pintuck the remaining fleece, sewing pintucks on the lengthwise straight of grain (direction of least stretch). Sew the first pintuck row. Using a quilt bar, edge guide, or spacer bar, sew the remaining pintucks 3/4" apart.

12. With pintucked fleece and pattern pieces right side up, cut out the herringbone sections. Place the drawn bias line precisely on top of a pintuck welt. (This will result in a perfect pintuck match-up at the seamlines, creating the herringbone angles.)

13. With right sides together, sew the herringbone sections together. Use a conventional sewing machine and sew with 3/8" seam allowances.

Nancy's Hints

#1 *When pinning the sections right sides together, match the pintucks by inserting a pin through the pintuck welt on the top layer and piercing the matching pintuck welt on the bottom layer.*

#2 *Since I want my pintucks to be perfectly matched, I first baste this seam to check the alignment. If I need to correct a pintuck or two, removing a few basting stitches is easy. When I'm happy with the pintuck alignment, I sew "for real."*

14. Finger press the seam allowances open and topstitch at 1/4". Remember to use a long 3.5mm or longer topstitch.

15. Complete the garment per the pattern directions.

Hooked on Pintucks!

The Totally Tucked Vest, a pattern from CNT Publishing, was intended to be made from a solid woven fabric. But...it is terrific made from fleece! This vest was made according to the pattern directions except that the armhole edges were finished with the quick and easy fat piping technique from Adventures With Polarfleece.

Or... looking at the world through "pintucked glasses."

This pattern is an example of what can happen when you look at a pattern with a different eye. Originally designed for muslin, denim, or woven cotton, it works beautifully with fleece!

Food for Thought:

(Or, this was my thought process to determine that this pattern would work in fleece. Use this same line of thinking when deciding whether any non-polar pattern would be suitable for fleece fabric.)

1. It was designed and sized with a little bulk in mind (the pattern calls for batting between the layers).

2. It has simple design lines.

3. High quality solid color fleece with little up-and-down stretch would not be subject to distortion from the pintucking.

4. Since fleece doesn't ravel, the armhole could be finished with the fat piping technique (an easy wrapped edge from *Adventures With Polarfleece*).

Chapter 4
CUTWORK ON FLEECE

Cutwork on fleece? Why not? Break the conventional rules! No longer restricted to heirloom sewing or dressy garment applications, cutwork on fleece opens up a whole new world of creativity.

Traditionally, cutwork has been found on woolen and linen couture garments as well as elegant bed and table linens. With new technology, high tech fabrics, crossover uses of fabrics, and most importantly, our adventuresome sewing nature...cutwork comes to fleece!

Cutwork on fleece is easy because fleece is a knit and knits don't ravel. And knits are very forgiving.

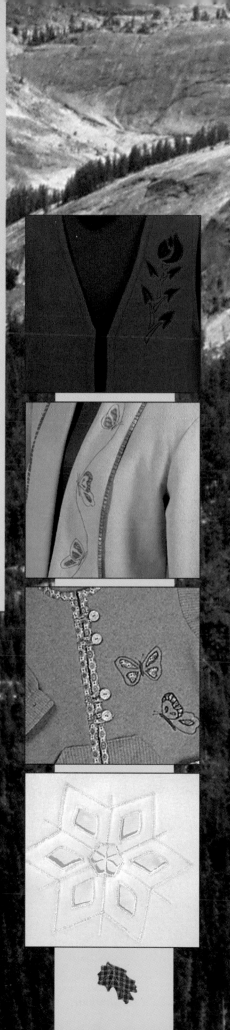

Great Places to Use Cutwork

Since cutwork involves cutout open areas, it is most suitable to use on garments that will not be subjected to heavy use or frequent laundering. Use cutwork to dress up your favorite jacket or vest pattern.

Cutwork looks great on:
→ Shawl collars
→ Cuffs
→ Vest fronts
→ Pockets
→ Hems
→ Centered down a jacket sleeve
→ Hat bands
→ Yokes
→ Even pillow tops!

Getting Started

Fleece Considerations

Just as if you were doing cutwork on a woven fabric, you need to choose a fleece fabric appropriate for the technique. Since cutwork is done on a single layer of fabric, you need a fleece that will stand up to your demands.

Choose a higher quality, medium to heavier weight dense fleece. You want it to be sturdy enough to withstand numerous procedures such as multiple stitchings, trimming, and removal of stabilizer. This is not the time to choose a wimpy fleece from the bargain table. If the fleece is skimpy and lacks body, it will not maintain a nice crisp edge.

Choose fleece with a tighter knit and a flat surface. Cutwork is not suitable for Berber or plush fabrics since their uneven texture will not allow a crisp even edge finish.

Where to Find Motif Ideas for Cutwork Designs

There are books and patterns devoted solely to cutwork designs. However, there are many other places to look for ideas:

→ Painting stencils
→ Quilting templates
→ Celtic designs
→ Appliqué books
→ Greeting cards
→ Wrapping paper
→ Computer clip art

What to Look for In a Design

Think simple. Since fleece garments are casual in nature, choose a simple casual design.

Those areas of the design that are stitched but left uncut are just as important, if not more so, than those areas that are actually cut away. Study traditional cutwork designs to get a feel for how the look and balance is accomplished. Simpler designs with fewer cutouts are more effective than intricate busy designs.

To get an idea of how a finished design will look, draw or trace the design with a pencil and shade in those areas you intend to cut away. Study the effect. Erase or add shaded areas until you have the look you like. (The rose motif is shown here at a reduced scale. The full-size template is on page 76.)

For the cutout areas to be visible and effective, they need to be a minimum of 1/2" x 1/2" in size. Tiny cutout areas are difficult to sew, difficult to trim, and not visually pleasing. As a general guide, most cutout areas are oblong, rectangular, or irregular in shape, a

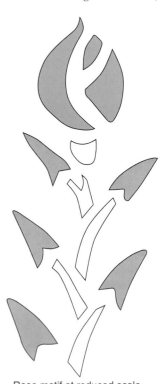

Rose motif at reduced scale

minimum of 1/2" wide and 1" or longer. (Experiment on a test sample to determine if the cutout area is appropriate.)

On the cutout areas that are immediately adjacent to each other, allow at least 1/4" fabric to remain between the cutout areas (3/8" is even better.) You need at least that much space between the cutout areas for support and to accommodate the satin stitching lines that will frame the cutout sections.

On some fleeces, if the cutout areas are larger than 1", you may need to add support bars to stabilize the open area. Support bars prevent "gap-osis" and stop the edges from fanning or curling.

If you like a design that is too small (like a motif taken from a greeting card) or too large (like one taken from a wall stencil), go to the local copy shop and enlarge or reduce the pattern as necessary.

A design from a greeting card or appliqué may have a nice look but be too intricate in its original form. Simplify it. Trace the dominant lines and eliminate unnecessary details. If necessary, add space to give ample room between areas that will be cut out. You may find that you draw and redraw three or four times until the motif feels just right. Shading in the areas to be cut out will help you visualize the finished look.

The butterfly example demonstrates how to modify and simplify a design to make it appropriate for cutwork.

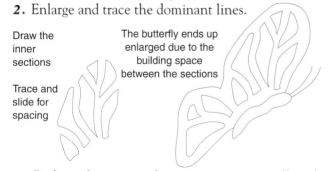

Original butterfly

Traced dominant lines and eliminated back wing

1. The original butterfly design has a nice overall look but is too small and too busy for cutwork.
2. Enlarge and trace the dominant lines.

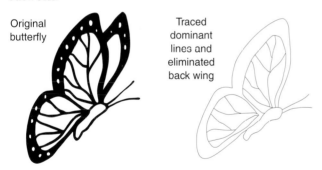

Draw the inner sections

The butterfly ends up enlarged due to the building space between the sections

Trace and slide for spacing

3. Redraw the potential cutout sections to allow for 1/4" to 3/8" space between areas. To obtain the necessary space between sections, trace a section and slide

the paper to trace the next section. This procedure enlarges the overall design. If necessary, it can be reduced at the local copy shop.
4. The redrawn butterfly still has too many sections in the inner wing.
5. Combine the inner wing sections until you have a look and balance you like.

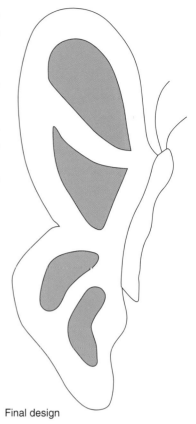

Final design

The three snowflake designs on page 64 were taken from clip art (readily available in printed form and in computer software format). Take note of the "before" (the original design) and the "after" (showing modifications done to adapt it for cutwork purposes).

Snowflake #1: The before (solid lines) was simple, but the inner diamonds were a little too small to make an effective cutwork statement. Simply enlarging the inner diamonds (the broken lines), ensuring at least 1/4" space between the cutout areas, made for a much more dramatic snowflake.

Snowflake #2: I loved the feel of this snowflake but the numerous spokes would entail too many stops and starts, requiring tying off too many thread tails. Plus the inner chambers were too small and too close to each other. After numerous redraws, I settled on enlarging the inner chambers just a little (planning to satin stitch with a narrower stitch width), and made continuous outer diamond loops for ease of stitching.

Snowflake #3: Beautiful and delicate, but I saw no logical way to adapt this design to cutwork. Since I intended the garment highlight to be a cascade of various snowflakes, I decided to simply sculpture stitch this snowflake design. However, the spoked ends still meant tedious tying off of thread tails. So I simply connected the spokes to each other, resulting in a delicate snowflake with lots of easy continuous stitching.

Snowflake #1
The solid lines are the
original design.
The broken lines are the
widened diamond opening.

Snowflake #2
This clip art
snowflake
redrawn became
this snowflake

Snowflake #3
This clip art became the design above for sculpturing

Nancy's Hints

#1 *For your first project, choose a thread color that blends with the fabric. It is very forgiving and looks beautiful on the first try. Traditionally, the finishing satin stitching on cutwork is done with a thread color that matches or is slightly darker than the fabric. The satin stitching blends beautifully with the fabric and looks nice and clean. Slight "hiccups" (mis-stitches, irregularities, uneven stitches) are hardly noticeable when the thread color blends with the fabric.*

#2 *If drama is more your style and a strong contrast thread is your choice, realize that every mis-step and hiccup will glare at you as you stitch. Don't be too hard on*

yourself and get distracted with every little irregularity. Finish the design. You'll be pleasantly surprised. The "whole" looks lovely, and the little mis-steps along the way are not as noticeable as you thought they would be.

#3 *Since the underside of traditional cutwork is frequently visible, traditional cutwork uses the same thread in the needle and in the bobbin. However, in most cutwork on fleece applications, the underside will never be seen. In this case, you may use matching colored regular sewing thread in your bobbin. This makes it easier to tie off the thread tails because then both threads are not slippery.*

Threads for Cutwork

Thread colors that match or are slightly darker than the fabric lend a subtle tone to cutwork. Strong contrasting colored thread offers a dramatic effect.

Regular thread will be used both for garment construction and the first steps of stabilizing the fleece for the cutwork procedures. Choose a high quality, long staple polyester thread that matches the fabric color.

Rayon thread in a 30 or 40 weight is the most popular choice for the finishing satin stitching. The lovely sheen offers a pretty edge finish. Rayon thread is heavier and smoother than regular thread, resulting in better, more even coverage. The color range available is tremendous. Use an embroidery needle for best results.

Metallic thread adds sparkle to the edge finish, but is a little fussier to stitch with. Be sure to use a specialty metallic needle, size 90/14, and have needle lubricant on hand for smoother stitching.

Sliver - ribbon-like polyester film threads - are metalized with aluminum to give them wonderful reflective characteristics. They offer a pretty edge finish but can be temperamental to stitch with and are recommended for the seasoned sewer.

When using Sliver:

1. Use a size 90/14 metallic or embroidery needle.
2. Loosen the upper tension to help the thread feed smoothly and lay flatter.
3. Make sure the thread is placed on a vertical spool pin. (The spool needs to rotate as the thread pulls off. This keeps the thread feeding flat through your machine and discourages twisting.)
4. Sew slowly (this is not a "pedal-to-the-metal" operation).
5. For easiest stitching, use matching regular or rayon thread in the bobbin. Take extra care to secure the thread ends at the beginning and end of the stitching.
6. Because Sliver is a "springy" thread, a dab of Fray Check on the tied thread tails is a good idea.

Needles for Cutwork

You will change needles throughout the various stages of sewing your garment. Construction is done with a universal needle. If, at various stages of construction, you find yourself stitching on multiple layers of fleece, you may need to change to a larger size needle to accommodate the bulk and prevent skipped stitches or needle breakage. When you change to a decorative thread for the cutwork satin stitching, change to a needle appropriate for your thread choice.

Universal 90/14 needle: This is the standard choice for garment construction and stabilizing stitch-

ing. If your fabric is a little lighter weight, you may opt to use a size 80/12. If your fabric is on the heavier side, you may choose a size 100/16. I find that size 90/14 is chosen the majority of the time.

Embroidery needle: For rayon thread. The larger eye and deeper groove allow for a smoother flow of the heavier thread. (Rayon thread is heavier than standard sewing thread.)

Metallic needle: For metallic threads. The larger eye, Teflon coating, and deeper groove accommodate the rougher surface of metallic thread with less shredding and breaking.

Other Notions for Cutwork

Totally Stable: This iron-on, tear-away temporary stabilizer serves two purposes. First, to trace the cutwork design. Second, to iron it on the wrong side of the fleece to add stability for the multiple stitchings and trimmings.

Solvy: A water-soluble film used as a base for stitching support bars and for completing the cutwork satin stitching.

KK2000 Spray Adhesive: A temporary adhesive used to adhere Solvy to the fleece. It does not gum up the needle or stiffen the fabric. The adhesive completely disappears, leaving no residue.

Scissors: Use high quality sharp scissors with good points for close accurate trimming. Appliqué or embroidery scissors are both good choices.

Fabric Erase Marker: Use to draw support bars on the Solvy.

Open Toe Embroidery or Appliqué Presser Foot: An open toe embroidery foot is the preferred presser foot because the open space between the toes offers excellent visibility. The wide groove on the underside of the embroidery or appliqué foot provides clearance for the satin stitch density to feed through easily.

Cutwork Effects

See-Through Cutwork: Cutwork done on a single layer of fleece.

Examples: If cutwork is done on an unlined vest front, the color of the shirt worn underneath would show through. If see-through cutwork were done on a single-layer, turn-back shawl collar, the self-fabric of the base garment would show through the cutout areas. The red vest with the rose shows see-through cutwork.

Self-Fabric Backed Cutwork: Cutwork done on the top layer of a double-layer area of the garment.

Examples: This would be on a traditional shawl collar (with upper collar and under collar) or lapel (with garment layer and facing), a roll-up cuff, a pocket facing, or a hem. The cutwork is sewn on the single, visible layer before garment construction. When the garment is built, the under layer peeks through the cutwork. The flower circle motif on the cuffs of the magenta pullover is an example of self-fabric backed cutwork. The flower circle on the center front is sculptured.

Nancy's Hints

#1 *Be aware that the **wrong side** of your fabric will show through the cutwork. Make sure the color or surface texture looks good. If not, use the stained glass cutwork technique (see below).*

#2 *Before sewing the cutwork design on the visible layer, pin baste that section of the garment together to make sure the seam allowances, seams, or other unwanted construction details won't surprise you and peek through the cutout areas.*

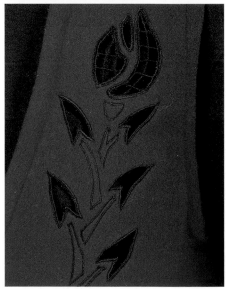

Stained Glass Cutwork (accent-backed): Unlike see-through and self-fabric backed cutwork, stained glass cutwork actually uses an accent fabric inserted behind the cutout areas. It permanently backs cutout areas because it is incorporated into the stitching.

Example: A cutwork flower or butterfly motif using a pretty woven cotton print inserted behind the cutout areas. The cotton print becomes the flower petals or butterfly wings. The butterflies on the lavender jacket show stained glass cutwork.

Nancy's Hint

If you like the subtle tone-on-tone effect of the self-fabric backed cutwork, but find that your construction details show through the cutout areas, use a piece of your matching lining fabric and the stained glass technique. The lining maintains the subtle tone-on-tone look, while the stained glass technique blocks out construction details. (This technique was used for the cream snowflake cardigan on the cover of this book.)

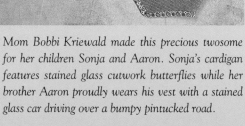

Mom Bobbi Kriewald made this precious twosome for her children Sonja and Aaron. Sonja's cardigan features stained glass cutwork butterflies while her brother Aaron proudly wears his vest with a stained glass car driving over a bumpy pintucked road.

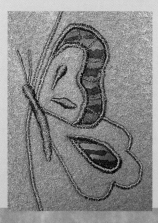

Cutwork Plan of Attack

If you are like me, before I get down to the nitty-gritty details of a project, I like to have a basic "road map" of where I am going before I proceed through the various steps. Following that train of thought, here are the simple "Basic Cutwork Directions" immediately followed by the "Detailed Cutwork Directions." The detailed directions are an elaboration of the basics, including hints, helps, suggestions, ideas, and things to consider.

Nancy's Hint

*To insure success, **always** do a cutwork test sample before you tackle the real project. Take this opportunity to experiment with different threads, tensions, and stitch densities to fine tune your work until your have exactly the look you want.*

Use the exact fabric, needle size and type, thread, and design you will use in your finished project. Completely read through the detailed directions. As you perfect your work, write down the machine adjustments you make as a reference for later. That way, if you do your sewing over a couple of days, you'll have the same adjustments at your fingertips.

Basic Cutwork Directions – The Road Map

1. Trace the design on Totally Stable.
2. Determine the arrangement of the motifs.
3. Press the traced Totally Stable against the wrong side of the fabric.
4. Using a short stitch length, straight stitch the design.
5. Trim away the cutout areas close to the stitching lines.
6. Zigzag stitch the edges of the cutout areas.
7. Spray KK2000 adhesive spray on the Totally Stable behind the cutout areas and adhere Solvy.
8. Stitch the support bars if necessary.
9. If doing stained glass cutwork, use KK2000 and adhere the contrast fabric behind the cutout areas.
10. Satin stitch around all the cut edges.
11. If doing stained glass cutwork, trim the excess contrast fabric.
12. Remove stabilizers.

Detailed Cutwork Directions

1. Trace the cutwork design on the wrong (papery) side of the Totally Stable.
a) Clearly mark those areas that are to be cut out. Using a pencil to shade in those areas works well.
b) Be aware that your *finished* design will be the reverse of your *traced* design. If your design has a definite right and left side, flip the design over and trace "backwards."

Nancy's Hints

Traced motif

Right side   Left side

Finished motif

#1 *If your design has a definite right or left side, you will need to think backwards. If, when you hold the design against the right side of your garment, the design is exactly how you want it, you will need to trace it backwards. (This is because you checked the design by holding it against the right side of the fabric but will be applying it to the wrong side of the fabric.) An easy way to do this is to use a light box or a sunny window. Simply flip the original design over to reverse the direction and trace.*

#2 *If tracing right or left image designs, label them as right or left according to their position on the garment as you're wearing it. This will avoid potential confusion or errors later.*

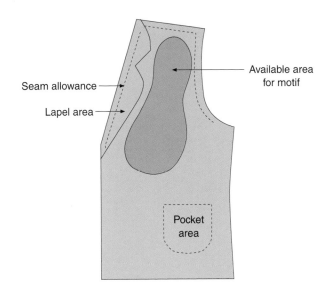

Seam allowance

Lapel area

Available area for motif

Pocket area

c) Set the iron temperature appropriate for polyester.

4. Straight stitch outline the entire design. With regular thread in the needle and bobbin and normal tension setting, straight stitch all the design lines drawn on the Totally Stable. Use a short 1.5mm to 2mm stitch length. Since you will be stitching over this a number of times, there is no need to do the usual backtacking to secure beginning and ending stitches. (This stitching accomplishes two things. First, it lends stability to the design and prevents stretching in those areas that will be cut away. Second, it stitch transfers the entire design to the right side of the fabric as a guide for later sculpture stitching.)

5. Cut out the designated areas. Using sharp scissors, trim away areas that are to be cut out (shaded areas in the traced design), trimming very close to the stitching. The remaining fleece next to the stitching line will later be completely covered with the satin stitching, so trim close and even.

6. Loosely zigzag stitch the cutout areas to provide additional strength to the cut edges. With regular thread still in the needle and bobbin and normal

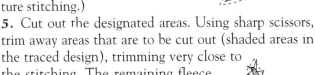

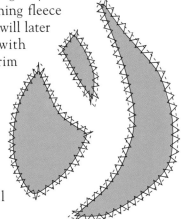

2. Decide how the motifs will be arranged. To determine the amount of space available for motifs:
a) Pin baste the seams and hems in the affected area.
b) Pin mark the topstitching lines.
c) Pin mark any unsuitable garment areas (pockets, pocket facings, collars, facings, cuff turn-back, etc.).
d) If the motif will be on a lapel collar, pin mark the fold line, seam allowances, and topstitching lines to see the amount of available space for the motif placement.
e) If the motif will be on the shoulder between the collar and the armscye, pin mark the armscye seam allowance and the placement for the finished edge of the collar to see the amount of available space for the motif placement.
f) If doing see-through or self-fabric backed cutwork, make sure no facing or construction details will show through.
g) In front of a mirror, hold the garment up to your body and determine flattering placement for the motif. (Don't skip this simple step - better safe than sorry.)
3. Press the traced Totally Stable against the *wrong* side of the fabric, arranging the design as determined in the above steps.
a) Place the slick (adhesive) side of the Totally Stable against the wrong side of the fabric and press with a dry iron.
b) Don't let the iron come in direct contact with the fleece. The iron should touch only the stabilizer.

tension settings, zigzag stitch around the trimmed edges using an open zigzag stitch. Set your machine for a 2.5mm stitch width and a 1mm stitch length. Center the zigzag stitching over the straight stitching line. If you are having trouble seeing your straight stitching line because it sinks into the loft of the fleece, try zigzag stitching from the wrong side. Trim any resulting "eyelashes" (those little fuzzies that poke out from the zigzagged and trimmed edges).

Note: If you are doing stained glass cutwork, incorporating contrast fabric to show through the cutout areas and you are not stitching any support bars, skip steps 7 and 8 and go directly to step 9.

7. Spray KK2000 temporary adhesive on the Totally Stable (on the underside of the fleece), spraying around the cutout areas. Adhere a piece of Solvy (to provide a base for sewing the support bars and the finishing satin stitching).

a) Place the fleece with the cutwork design right side down on a flat surface and slip a piece of paper underneath the cutout areas to protect the tabletop from the adhesive spray.

b) Lightly spray the adhesive on the Totally Stable, spraying only that area that will be covered with Solvy.

Nancy's Caution

If you spray the adhesive on the Solvy instead of the Totally Stable, there will be adhesive on the Solvy in the cutout areas. When stitching the support bars and the finishing satin stitching, the tackiness of the adhesive will interfere with the presser foot gliding smoothly.

8. Stitch support bars if necessary. Support bars are thread ropes from cut edge to cut edge, crossing larger open areas to prevent the edges from flaring or distorting. Support bars provide stability for larger open cutout areas that cannot maintain their shape independently. The weight and stability of your fleece plus the openness of your design will dictate the need for support bars.

Nancy's Hint

If in doubt as to whether your design needs support bars, add them! They are easy to do and add lovely detailing to any design. Personally, I always do the heavy support bars. The coarse crocheted look complements the fleece.

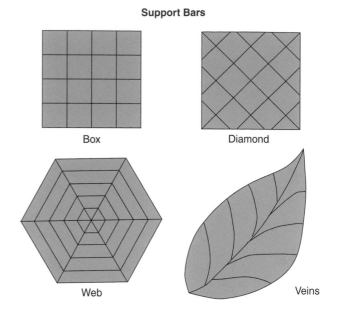

Support Bars

Box

Diamond

Web

Veins

a) Use a fabric marker to draw the support bar lines on Solvy. Arrange the support bars to complement your design. Veins are a great accent for leaves, webs work well in curved designs, geometric designs favor a box or diamond scheme, and straight lines work well in all motifs.

b) Place decorative thread in the needle. Depending on the thread chosen, place matching decorative thread in your bobbin or keep regular thread in the bobbin. (Sew a test sample on Solvy and see if regular bobbin thread looks okay. If your decorative thread is a temperamental one, sewing may be easier with regular thread in the bobbin.)

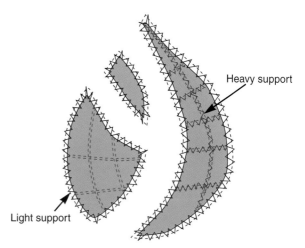

Heavy support

Light support

c) **Light Support Bars**: Using a 1.5mm straight stitch, stitch across each drawn line, being careful to solidly anchor and backtack each end in the straight stitch outline. Stitch again, exactly on top of the first stitching (double row of straight stitches).

d) **Heavy Support Bars**: Begin the same as for light support bars (straight stitching lines sewn twice).

Then cover the double straight stitch lines with a zigzag stitch 1mm wide x 1.5mm long (this zigzag stitch results in a crocheted rope look).

9. If doing stained glass cutwork (backing the cutout areas with contrast fabric), adhere the backing fabric behind the cutout areas.

a) If the cutout areas don't have support bars, lightly spray KK2000 temporary adhesive on the Totally Stable on the underside of the fleece. Place the fleece with the cutwork design right side down on a flat surface and slip a piece of paper under the cutout areas to protect the tabletop from the adhesive spray.

b) If the cutout areas have support bars, lightly spray KK2000 temporary adhesive on the Solvy.

c) With the right side of the contrast fabric against the wrong side of the garment, adhere contrast fabric behind the cutout areas. The contrast fabric just needs to be large enough to back the cutout areas. The excess will be trimmed away.

10. On the right side of the fabric, satin stitch around all the open cutwork edges, securing the beginning and ending stitches. Fray Check if necessary.

a) If doing stained glass cutwork with a contrast fabric backing the open cutwork, the satin stitch finishing will attach the contrast fabric to the fleece.

b) Place decorative thread in the needle, changing to an appropriate needle type for your chosen thread. If the underside of your cutwork is unlikely to be visible, you can use regular thread in the bobbin. If it will be visible, use decorative thread in the bobbin.

c) Set the zigzag stitch for a 3mm to 3.5mm width and a length appropriate to provide a nice fill (refer to your test sample information). A too-loose stitch density is better than a too-tight density. Your stitch length is too short if the fleece needs to be helped through. A too-tight stitch density will result in wavy cutwork edges.

d) Referring to your test sample, loosen the upper tension so the top stitches pull slightly to the underside.

e) To easily blend beginning and ending stitches, start the satin stitching in the middle of a long edge rather than at a corner or point on the motif.

f) Begin the finishing stitches by straight stitching backwards for 1/2", using a short stitch length. Stop. Clip

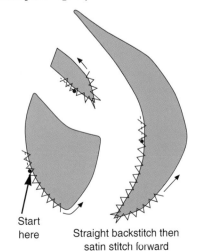

Start here

Straight backstitch then satin stitch forward

the thread tails. Change to a zigzag stitch, then satin stitch forward, covering the beginning stitches. (This method secures the beginning stitches. At the same time, it avoids having to tie off the beginning thread tails and eliminates excess thread buildup that back-tacking would cause.)

g) When stitching, be careful to keep the stitches at a right angle to the design's cut edges.

h) Make sure the zigzag satin stitches completely cover the cut edges of the design. The majority of the stitch should fall on the fabric. The swing of the zigzag stitch should fall over the cut edge of the cutout area onto the Solvy or contrast backing fabric.

i) When stitching around curves, pay close attention when you shift the angle of your fabric to maintain smooth even coverage. Avoid gaps and misses by making sure each pivot stitch covers the previous one. (Use standard appliqué stitching techniques for curves, making sure the pivot of the stitch is always on the widest side of the curve.)

j) Easy block corners or mitered corners provide the most strength for cutout areas. The tapered corner, while beautiful on appliqués, is too weak to frame a cutout corner.

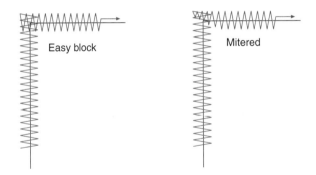

Easy block   Mitered

Easy Block Corner: Like it sounds, this method involves no changing of stitch width. Simply satin stitch a little beyond the corner, ending on the outside of the zigzag swing. Pivot at a 90° angle and continue satin stitching. The result is a blunt squared point or corner.

Mitered Corner: The mitered corner begins the same as the easy block in that you satin stitch slightly beyond the corner, ending on the outside of the zigzag swing. Pivot at a 90° angle, then set the stitch *width* to 0. Increase the stitch width as you sew the second side of the point. The graduated overlapping of stitches results in a mitered look. (*Caution:* If your machine gives a stair step rather than a smooth taper, choose the easy block method.)

k) Think landscaping. When completing the finishing satin stitching, plan your order of stitching from the background toward the foreground. The reasoning is both practical and aesthetically pleasing. It's practical because if you plan which stitching lines will cross which lines, you can eliminate the need to tie off some beginning and ending stitches since they will be buried under later satin stitch lines. And it's attractive - besides adding depth and dimension, it is pleasing to the eye when the upper layers are actually on top of the under layers. Example: The butterfly on the vine illustration shows landscape thinking. I used varied satin stitch widths for interest, dimension, and balance. I chose 3mm as the widest stitch (rather than 3.5mm or 4mm) to enhance the more delicate feel of butterflies. The vine is a little narrower stitch width (2mm to 2.5mm). The delicate antennae were stitched with a fine 1.5mm stitch width.

Butterfly Stitching Order: The cutout (shaded) area on the upper wing has already been stabilized with support bars and contrast backing fabric (if used) has already been adhered in place.

k-1) Using a 3mm stitch width, satin stitch the inner edge of the upper wing and outer edge of the lower wing. The stitching ends don't need to be secured since subsequent stitchings will cover and secure them. Satin stitch the teardrop on the lower wing, securing the beginning and ending stitches. On the upper wing, make sure to adequately cover the ends of the support bars.

k-2) Satin stitch the vine with a narrow width (2mm to 2.5mm). If you will be filling in the butterfly body with graduated machine satin stitching, you may continue stitching the vine through the body since it will be covered by the satin fill. If you are simply satin stitching the border of the body, stop the vine stitching at the body. Tie off the threads at the vine ends by pulling thread tails to the underside and tying off to secure.

k-3) Satin stitch the antennae with a 1.5mm narrow

width. Pull through and tie off the thread tails at the antennae ends. The other ends will be buried under the stitching of the body.

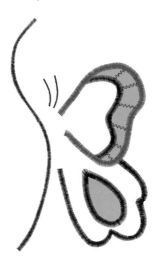

k-4) Using a 3mm stitch width, satin stitch the outer edge of the upper wing. Be sure to adequately cover the stitching ends of the inner wing and lower wing, as well as adequately cover the ends of the support bars. The beginning and end don't need to be secured since the body stitching will cover them.

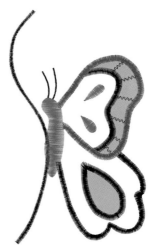

k-5) Set the stitch width at 0. Beginning at the tail, satin stitch fill the body, gradually altering the stitch width to fill the body. Or satin stitch outline the body at a 2mm stitch width, covering the vine ends and wing ends. Secure the beginning and ending stitches.

k-6) Set the stitch width at 0. Beginning at the points, gradually alter the stitch width to fill the small teardrops. Secure the stitches at the beginning and end of the stitching.

11. Trim the backing fabric (if used) close to the stitching.

12. Remove stabilizers.

Cutwork Gallery

The Snowflake cardigan showcases a variety of techniques featured throughout the book. The stained glass cutwork uses the lining as a backing. The delicate sculptured snowflakes sparkle with iridescent Sliver thread. The very subtle snowflakes are simply the first step of stitch transferring. Snowflake templates are on pages 74-75.

Enlarge or reduce as desired

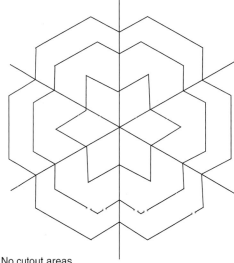

No cutout areas
Sculpture or stitch transfer only

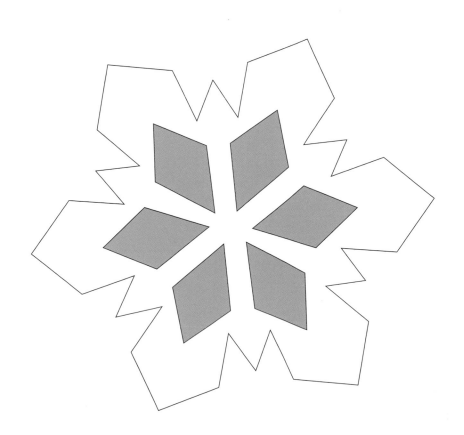

Single Rose Template

Butterfly Templates

Satin stitch fill in the bodies and teardrop accents

Pansy in Circle Template

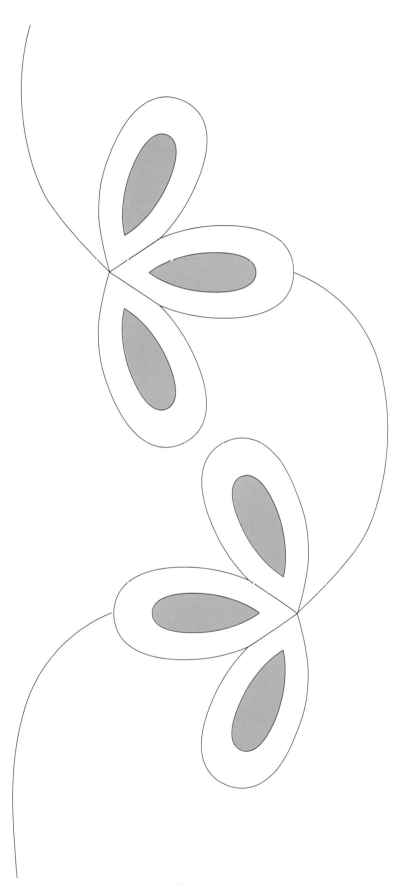

Flower Wave Template

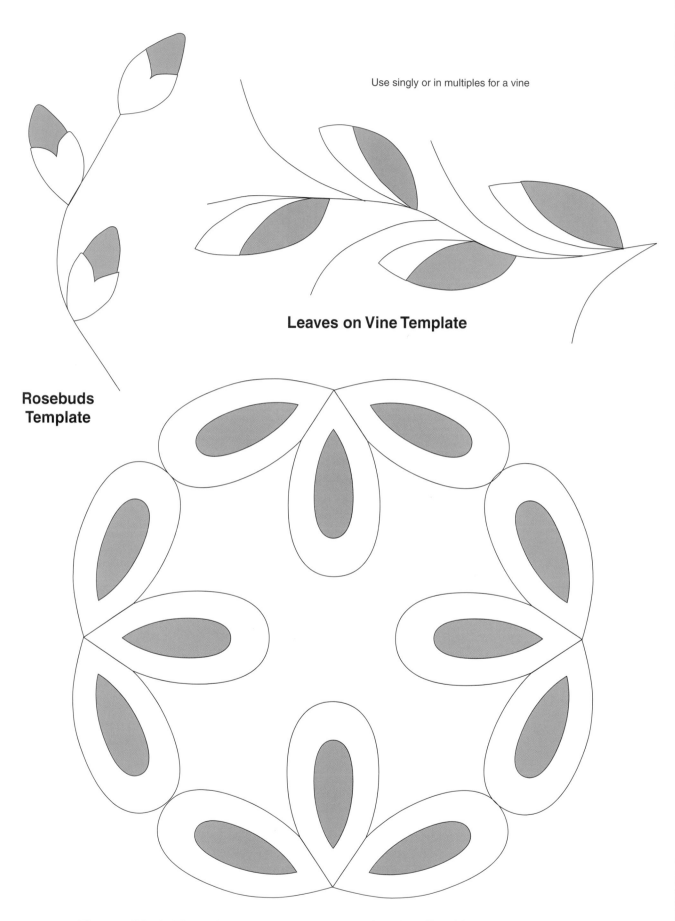

Use singly or in multiples for a vine

Leaves on Vine Template

Rosebuds Template

Flower Circle Template

See this motif used for sculpturing and cutwork on page 67

Satin stitch fill in
teardrop accents

Tulips Template

Daisy Swirl Template

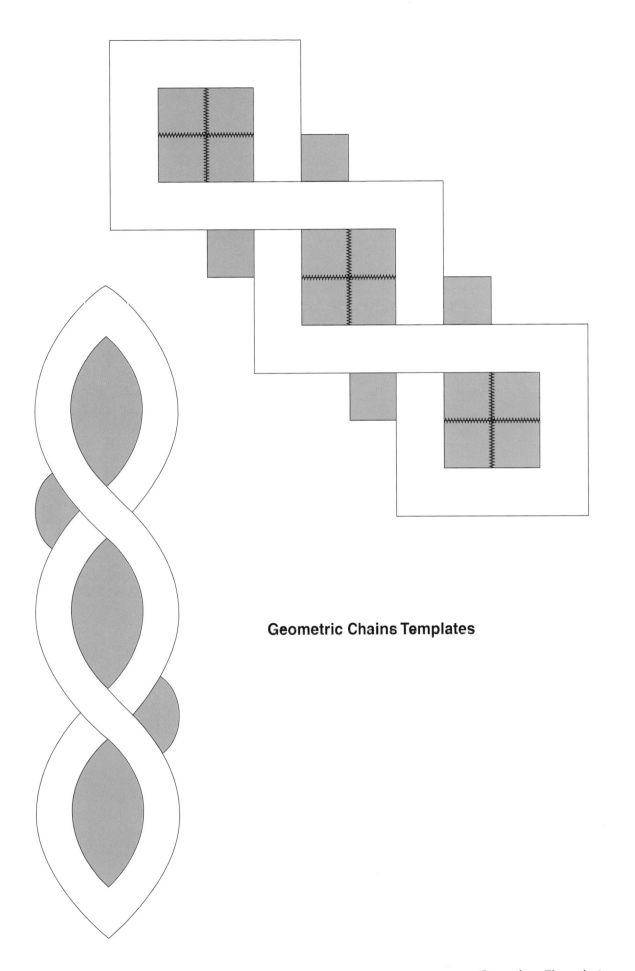

Geometric Chains Templates

Autumn Leaves Templates

These leaves are lovely with heavy support bars, backed with a cotton print.

Chapter 5

EMBROIDERY ON FLEECE

High tech fabrics combined with high tech computerized sewing machines offer today's home sewer the opportunity to create designs previously found only in the ready-to-wear market.

Machine embroidery has exploded onto the sewing scene and has added a fun new element to sewing.

Machine embroidery on fleece opens up a whole new world of creative possibilities for the home sewer. Before beginning to embroider on fleece, you need to consider the same factors that would affect any embroidery project. Take into account your fabric and thread choices when determining the appropriate needle type and size, as well as stabilization needs. Embroidering on fleece is as easy as sewing on fleece. It is quite forgiving. However, Polarfleece, Berbers, and plush fabrics toss in a few new variables to the embroidery equation.

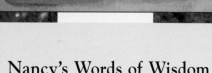

Nancy's Words of Wisdom

After you've read through this section and have your machine all set up and ready to go, take the time to do an embroidery test sample first! You don't have to complete the entire design, but do stitch enough to see if you are happy with the end result or if you need to make some adjustments. It's definitely a worthwhile investment of time to save frustration and possible do-overs.

Food for thought: While you are embroidering your test samples, keep in mind the potential they offer. Read the embroidered coaster idea on page 94 for putting your test pieces to good use.

First Things First

Thread

For the best coverage and most pleasing visual effect, choose threads specifically designated for embroidery. Rayon in 30 or 40 weight is the most popular and readily available thread choice. Rayon threads offer a large color range, provide a lovely sheen, and give better thread coverage because they are heavier than normal construction sewing thread.

Metallic thread offers another excellent decorative option. Use lightweight thread in the bobbin. Using needle lubricant and a size 90/14 metallic needle helps reduce metallic thread shredding and breakage. Check your embroidery machine manual to see if a needle lubricant can be used with your machine.

There are many threads available and more are constantly being introduced. I only mention rayon and metallic since they are the most commonly used and readily available.

Needles - Type & Size

Type: For best stitch quality and fill-in, choose the appropriate needle *type* for the thread you are using. Choose embroidery needles for 40 weight rayon thread. Choose metallic needles when using metallic threads or heavier 30 weight rayon thread. The needle eyes and grooves are designed to accommodate the size and special characteristics of these threads.

Size: Choose needle *size* according to the weight of the fabric you are embroidering - size 75/11 and 80/12 for lighter weights; size 90/14 for mid-weights; size 100/16 for heavyweights. You want to use the smallest size needle that will not deflect when penetrating the fabric and that will make a large enough hole to pass the thread through without breaking. When sewing with metallic thread, a size 90/14 metallic needle provides the best results.

Nancy's Reminder

Change needles often! Since you personally are not doing any of the work, it may not seem like you are doing much stitching. But embroidery designs use thousands and thousands of stitches! The minute you experience poor stitch quality or thread breakage, change the needle! It's probably dull.

Fabric Challenges & Solutions

Challenge: Bulky fleece and pile fabrics are difficult to hoop. Plus, hooping may leave unwanted hoop imprints on the fleece.

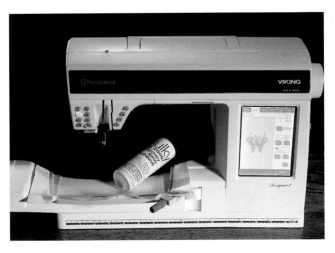

Solution #1 (preferred technique): Hoop a medium weight stabilizer (tear-away or cut-away, whichever you prefer) and lightly spray the tautly hooped stabilizer with Sulky KK2000 temporary adhesive. Lay the fleece on the exposed tacky stabilizer and finger press in place.

Solution #2: Hoop one of the adhesive papers available on the market instead of hooping the fabric. Remove the protective paper to reveal the adhesive and adhere the fleece in place.

Note #1: Hooping the adhesive paper simply replaces hooping your fabric, it *does not* replace the need for stabilization. You still need to insert stabilizer under the hoop.

Note #2: It is not necessary to rehoop adhesive paper after each design. You can cut a new piece and patch the hole!

Nancy's Caution

Adhere gently, sticking only the immediate area to be embroidered. When removing the leftover adhesive paper, it tends to de-fleece the fabric. On some fleeces this may result in weak or bare spots. It's a good idea to test how adhesive paper will react on your chosen fleece. Leave adhesive paper adhered to the fabric the shortest length of time possible. Adhere, embroider, remove. Adhesives are designed to get stronger the longer they are in contact. The quicker you remove it, the easier the removal process.

Challenge: Getting even thread coverage throughout the design. Embroidered designs may result in uneven coverage due to the lofty and often uneven fabric surfaces found on Polarfleece, Berbers, and plush fabrics. You may find unwanted fleece hairs peeking through between the stitches or Berber bumps pushing stitches aside.

Solution: Use a "topping" on the top of your fabric. A topping is a stabilizer that acts as a go-between layer between the stitches and the fabric, allowing the stitches to stay where they are put. Solvy, a water-soluble film, is the most popular choice because it easily tears away after stitching the design. If a heavier topping is needed, Super Solvy is double weight. If there is any leftover Solvy visible around the stitches, it can be rinsed away.

To use Solvy as a topping, cover the design area with Solvy. Pin in place or spray KK2000 on the Solvy and adhere the Solvy to the fleece.

Challenge: Show through. Show through occurs when the thread color strongly contrasts with the base fabric color and the base color shows through the stitched design.

Stars on the left were embroidered with no topping. The center stars show embroidery using Solvy as a topping. The stars on the right show finished embroidered stars with the excess Solvy torn away.

Example: A stark white polar bear embroidered on a bright red fleece. The red background may allow hints of red to show through the white threads. This can happen even though stitch density is correct, enough stabilizer is used, and a Solvy topping is used. It's a fact of life that white thread is not strong enough to block out the red background.

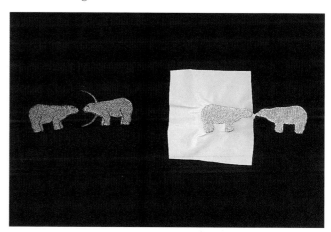

Solution: Use Cover-Up as a topping instead of the water-soluble film. Cover-Up is a permanent, plastic vinyl stabilizer from Hoop-It-All, Inc. It comes in a variety of solid colors, with or without adhesive backing. Match the Cover-Up color to the thread color. Cut a piece of Cover-Up slightly larger than the area you need to embroider and pin or adhere in place. Stitch that color area of the design. Before continuing other areas of the design, tear away the unstitched portion of the Cover-Up and discard. (As with all adhesives, if using the adhesive-backed Cover-Up, leave it adhered to the fabric the shortest time possible.)

Stabilizers & Stitch Quality

Embroidery on fleece, like embroidery on any type of fabric, requires adequate stabilization for the design to fill nicely without gaps and for the outline stitching to be aligned perfectly. If the quality of your test sample falls short of your expectations, and presuming you have a fresh needle of appropriate size and type, inadequate stabilization is probably the culprit.

Generally speaking, the heavier the stabilization you use, the better the stitching. Since you don't want a rock-hard backing on your design, it now becomes a game of balance to use just enough stabilization to get good stitching but not too much as to overpower the comfort and looks of the garment.

If using a tear-away stabilizer, it's better to use multiple layers of mid-weight stabilizers for additional stabilization than one heavyweight stabilizer. Using multiple layers allows you to tear away one layer at a time.

This is much gentler on the stitches with less chance of distortion.

Again, always do a test sample first. This will give you all the information you need for a successful design.

Housekeeping

I know that sewing and creating magnificent wonders are supposed to take our minds off the drudgery of housekeeping, but our machines do need a little tender upkeep. Start your embroidery project with a cleaned, oiled machine. And when finished, clean and oil again. Lint buildup can interfere with the smooth movement of your machine. Lint and fleece fuzz absorb oil. Give your machine tender loving attention and it will repay you with lovely stitch quality.

Texturizing With Underlay Stitches

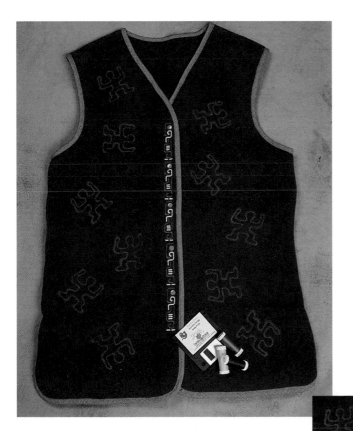

As I was finishing up the details for this book, Jeanine Twigg called me all excited to share her latest discovery. I took one look at the result and knew this clever idea had to be included in the book. Thanks Jeanine!

Jeanine Twigg - industry snap expert, inventor of the SnapSetter and founder of The Snap Source, Inc. which provides sewers with long-pronged snaps - is also a lover of sewing on fleece. While playing with machine embroidery on fleece, she was delightfully surprised to find that the underlay stitches of embroidery designs can offer wonderful texturizing opportunities when used on solid color fleece.

The design featured on Jeanine's vest is from Cactus Punch. The design was intended to be finished as a satin stitch motif. However, Jeanine found that the underlay stitches created eye-catching design outlines and stopped embroidering after this first step! These underlay stitches are similar to a three-step zigzag and provide just enough stitches to compress the fleece and create a textured outline. Therefore, it isn't necessary to stitch out the rest of the design. Just stitch the underlay portion and forget about the rest. It's fast, fun, and simple!

Underlay stitches are the first group of stitches that lay the groundwork for fill-in satin stitch designs. Their purpose is to stabilize the design area and hold the designs in shape.

Most designs have many parts to the embroidery process. Starts, stops, jumps, underlay stitches, running stitches, satin stitches, and more. By moving through a design on your embroidery machine or the program on your sewing machine, you can choose what portions of the design you'd like to stitch. Move through the design until you reach the underlay stitches.

All embroidery designs are created using a process called "digitizing." You can purchase designs on computer disks that are professionally digitized or you can create your own designs with the appropriate software on your home computer. Designs can be transferred to your embroidery equipment and stitched onto your fleece. If the underlay stitches on your chosen design don't offer a pretty outline for texturizing fleece...design your own!

Nancy's Note

The following is Jeanine's method for embroidering on fleece. Personally, I like hooping the stabilizer, adhering the fleece using KK2000 temporary adhesive spray, and topping with Solvy. Jeanine's approach is different. Try both and use the method you prefer.

Jeanine's Method

Hoop the fleece and Solvy together, using the Solvy as a topping (no other stabilizer is needed). Typically, fabric hooped for embroidery should be taut. Not so with fleece. Hoop it very lightly (the hoop merely serves as a holder for the fleece). *Do not tighten the hoop or pull on the stabilizer after the fleece is in the hoop.* When stitching the design, be sure that the fleece is resting completely on the table, not dangling off the edge. As with all embroidery projects, it's best to stitch a test sample first, before embroidering "for real."

Nancy's Afterthought

After thinking about Jeanine's idea for using only parts of the embroidery process, I got to thinking about the other ways to use "embroidery parts." This is probably just the beginning...

1. Combine cutwork embroidery designs with the information provided in the Cutwork chapter for easy cutwork on fleece.

2. Use just the outline stitching from embroidery quilting motifs to produce subtle impressions. (Remember how we used just the stitch transfer portion of a couple snowflakes in the cutwork design in Chapter 4? Same idea.)

3. Again, use just the outline stitching portion from embroidery quilting motifs combined with the blunt edge appliqué in reverse idea from Chapter 6. Choose a motif with a simpler outline that will provide good areas to trim away. Using your embroidery machine insures that all the motifs are identical.

4. Appliqué embroidery designs offer great outline underlays prior to the finishing satin stitching. Skip the appliqué. Skip the satin stitching. Just texturize with the underlay!

Shaving Berbers

Embroidery on Berbers is a very classy look. As outlined above, you will need a topping like Solvy to allow the stitches to lay smoothly alongside each other and to keep them from sinking into the loft of the pile.

If your Berber is too thick and lush to get a good-looking design, or just for the fun of it...shave it!

Using common household and sewing tools, you can shear a section of Berber to create a low-loft area for an embroidery design. Shear an area larger than the design so it serves as a shadowbox for the design. Whether it's a 1" or 2" perimeter around the design depends on the look you want.

1. Determine the finished size of the embroidered design and the amount of shaved area you want surrounding the motif.
2. Mark the design placement.
3. Shear the area.

a) I tried a variety of tools and they all worked. Some worked a little quicker and easier than others, but it shows that there is more than one way to approach this. I first tried hair clippers (they worked pretty well and I did ask permission of the men in the household first). Then I used appliqué scissors (also worked well, but I had to be careful to keep the area evenly cropped). Finally, I tried one of those little sweater shavers (it worked adequately but took quite a bit longer - not my first choice).

b) Experiment on a scrap first. Depending on the fabric and your choice of tools, you may work with the Berber held flat against a tabletop or try holding the Berber taut over something smooth like the rounded bottom of an upside-down bowl.

c) Shave and check. Shave and check. Repeat until you have the indent you want without shearing too closely to the base fabric as to show threads.

d) Some Berber colors will show the cropped area nicely while on other colors it will hardly be noticeable. That's another reason to do a test "shave" first.

4. Embroider the design using the stabilizing and topping techniques described on pages 89-91.

FOOD FOR THOUGHT:
Design Possibilities

Thumb through the different chapters in this book. Mix and match ideas, combining techniques to complement each other. Embroider on an appliqué. Pintuck a tic-tac-toe grid on a pullover top and embroider designs in every other box. Embroider a dramatic design and frame it with pintucks. Buy 1½ to 2 yards of plaid fleece in your favorite school's colors and embroider the school mascot on one corner to be in style for the football games. The potential is endless.

Bottom line…play and have fun!

Ada Robinson had fun using her embroidery machine to embroider tone-on-tone motifs as well as cutwork designs. Quick (she made the 30-minute vest from Adventures With Polarfleece) *and easy (her embroidery machine did all the work)!*

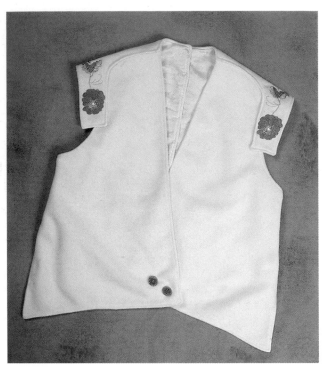
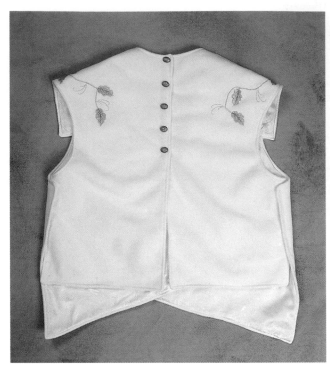

Sue Mitrovich chose metallic thread and a Jenny Haskins embroidery design to add the finishing touches to her stylish Lois Ericson vest.

Speaking of playing - use your test embroidery samples to make beautiful and practical coasters. When embroidering a motif, Golden Rule #1 says to first stitch a sample to check tensions and density. Great advice, but why waste all those test samples when they can be put to good use?

Coasters from Test Samples

Using test embroidery samples on fleece, create 4" x 4" square or round coasters. The cutting dimensions of the coasters are governed by how you are going to construct them.

Coasters can be finished a variety of ways:
1. With wrong sides together, stitch two layers of a fleece coaster with a 1/2" seam allowance. Using a straight or wavy edge rotary blade, trim the seam allowance 1/4" from the stitching line, leaving the wavy edge as a blunt edge decorative finish.
2. Sew the coaster right sides together with a 1/4" seam allowance. Leave a small opening for turning. Turn. Hand stitch the opening closed. Topstitch at 3/8".

3. Cut a single layer of fleece and adhere to a cork backing.
4. With wrong sides together, serger finish the outer edges using decorative threads in the loopers.

Chapter 6
APPLIQUÉ ON FLEECE

This chapter is fun because appliqué on fleece is so simple! New products on the market, new sewing machine technology, and new techniques have virtually eliminated any problems. Appliqué on fleece is fast, fun, and (best of all) easy!

Included in this chapter are six appliqué techniques - all easy. There is no one right way. The question is, "Which do you prefer?" The technique you choose will be governed by the choice of appliqué fabric used, along with the look you prefer.

Appliqués on most fabrics (other than fleece) are fused in place. This provides a nice smooth surface on which to satin stitch. However, fusing appliqués on fleece is a potentially risky business. There is the danger of flattening the nap, or even worse, melting the fleece. Neither of these disasters is recoverable.

Thanks to KK2000 temporary adhesive spray for coming to the rescue. It holds the appliqué firmly in place. No need for fusing. No gummy needles. No need to remove (the adhesive disappears over a few days). Couldn't be any easier!

So grab your fleece, an assortment of fabrics to make appliqués, decorative thread, and let's get started! After you've read through the appliqué techniques, you'll find templates and directions at the end of the chapter to play with. And you'll notice that they incorporate a variety of other techniques featured throughout the book.

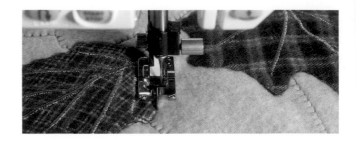

➜ Totally Stable (iron-on tear-away stabilizer)
➜ Sulky KK2000 (temporary spray adhesive)
➜ Decorative thread (for the needle)
➜ Appropriate needle (for the decorative thread chosen)
➜ Regular thread (for the bobbin)

*T*raditional Satin Stitch Edge Finish

Use this technique on any appliqué when you want the appliqué to have a smooth beaded satin stitch finished edge. The garment will first be stabilized to remove any possibility of distortion while satin stitching.

1. Press Totally Stable to the wrong side of the garment to stabilize the area behind the appliqué.
2. Cut out the appliqué motifs.
3. Lightly spray KK2000 on the wrong side of the appliqués and adhere them in place.
4. Thread an appropriate needle with rayon or metallic decorative thread. Loosen the needle tension so the stitches pull slightly to the underside. Keep regular thread in the bobbin. (*Note:* Clear or smoke thread may be used if a satin stitch without color is desired. Use a size 80/12 needle.)
5. For best visibility, choose a 3mm or wider zigzag stitch width. (Remember, this stitch will sink into the loft of the fleece a little bit.)

6. Shorten the stitch density enough to produce a nice satin stitch. Don't overly shorten the stitch length (a too-tight satin stitch packs too much thread into the fabric and encourages rippling when the Totally Stabilizer is removed).
7. When finished, remove the stabilizer and discard.

*B*lunt Edge Finish Appliqué

This easy technique is suitable when the appliqué fabric doesn't ravel. Perfect for appliqués made from fleece, Berber, UltraSuede, etc. Since the fabric doesn't ravel, there is no need to encase the edges.

For blunt edge appliqués cut from fleece, choose a medium to medium/heavyweight fleece so the blunt edges maintain their clean, sharp edge. While Berber doesn't fit the criteria of leaving a clean blunt edge, it gives wonderful depth and realism to animal appliqués like Scotty dogs, bunnies, lambs, etc. (Berber appliqués may be edgestitched or satin stitched in place.)

Unless the garment fabric is extremely stretchy, there is no need to stabilize the underside with Totally

Stable. Edgestitching doesn't build in the quantity of thread that satin stitching does. Unless the base fleece is very stretchy, distortion is minimal.

1. Cut out the appliqué motifs, leaving clean blunt edges.

2. Lightly spray KK2000 on the wrong side of the appliqué and adhere in place.

3. Thread an appropriate needle with regular, decorative, or clear thread. Keep regular thread in the bobbin.

4. Edgestitch the appliqué in place using a medium to longer straight stitch (3mm to 3.5mm).

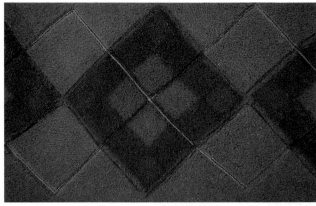

A combination of techniques complements the motif. The blunt edge argyle applique is accented with diamond sculpture stitching.

Nancy's Hint

For a no-hassle edgestitch, use your edgestitch presser foot and move the needle position to the right or left until the stitching line is about 1/8" from the raw edge.

*B*lunt Edge Appliqué– In Reverse!

For a fun variation of the blunt edge appliqué technique, do it in reverse. Using two layers of fleece in complementary contrasting colors, straight stitch a simple motif and trim away one layer to reveal the "reverse appliqué" peeking through!

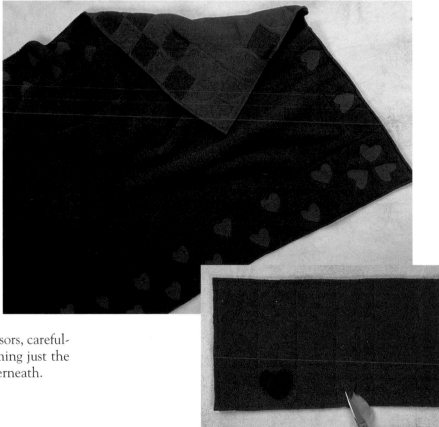

1. Place the fleeces *wrong* sides together.

2. Depending on what you are making and what stage of construction you are at, baste or stitch the outer edges of the layers together.

3. With matching threads in the needle and bobbin (two different colors, matching each fleece color), straight stitch around the motif. (See Nancy's Hint on page 98 for an easy way to outline stitch multiple motifs.)

4. Using sharp appliqué or embroidery scissors, carefully trim away the inside of the motif, trimming just the top layer to reveal the contrast fleece underneath.

The directions and template for the Heart Blanket are on page 103. See the Crusher Hat and Scarf ideas featured in Chapter 9, Scrap Happy, for more clever uses of blunt edge appliqué in reverse.

Dimensional Appliqué

If you have done dimensional appliqué using other fabrics, you are in for a delightful surprise when you apply this idea to fleece! Dimensional appliqué with fleece takes the blunt edge finish appliqué one step further. Combine it with other embellishment techniques for interest and contrast.

When Julie Muschamp showed me her periwinkle jacket, I knew it had to be pictured in the book! Julie, a Northwest sewing instructor and designer, fashioned a deep dramatic shawl collar, sculptured it with wavy lines (from the Sculpturing chapter), embellished it with black rickrack fleece trim (from the Finishing Touches chapter), and added depth with dimensional leaf appliqués.

October Branches, my rust tweed boucle pullover, combines strong bold sculpturing in the branches with dimensional leaves. Directions and templates for October Branches are given on page 104.

1. Cut out simple appliqué designs, leaving clean blunt edges. Good motif choices include leaves, flowers, flower petals, butterfly wings, etc.

2. To give shape, pinch and stitch a small dart at the base of the appliqué (base of leaf, bottom of flower petal, body edge of butterfly wing). Each motif will be different, depending on the size of the motif, the weight of the fleece, and how much you want it to crimp or buckle. A good starting point: on a medium motif, pinch 1/2" fabric to form a 1/4" dart. Stitch and trim the dart.

3. Sculpture stitch the inner details (leaf veins, flower creases, butterfly wing divisions), stitching over the dart as necessary.

Nancy's Note

In the Sculpturing chapter, the wrong side of the fabric was always stabilized with Totally Stable before sculpture stitching to prevent distortion. Not so here. Here you will sew incorrectly for a purpose. Any distortion from the sculpturing will add more realism to the appliqué!

4. Place the appliqué on the garment where desired. Scrunch up the appliqué to encourage it to buckle and give dimension to the motif and pin in place.

5. Secure the appliqué to the garment by spot stitching over or alongside the sculpture stitching lines, or mini bartacking at the base and tips. If spot stitching with matching thread will be visible, use clear monofilament thread instead. Tie off the thread tails securely to finish.

Blindhem Appliqué

This technique is a nice choice for soft woven cotton or flannel appliqués when you want a subtle hand-stitched look. You'll love the easy way to turn under and finish the raw edges of the appliqué. In addition to regular sewing supplies, you will need enough light-weight fusible interfacing to back the appliqués.

1. Place cutout appliqués on pieces of lightweight fusible interfacing, *right* sides together. (This is a great speed technique. There is no need to spend time cutting out interfacing appliqué shapes hoping they'll exactly match the appliqué pieces.)

2. Stitch around the entire appliqué using a short stitch length and a 1/8" seam allowance. Use regular thread and a shorter straight stitch length (2.5mm).

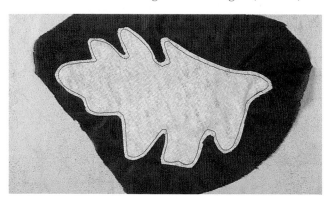

3. Trim the excess interfacing. Clip curves and points as necessary for ease in turning.

4. Cut a slit in the center of the interfacing only, stopping 1" from each seamline.

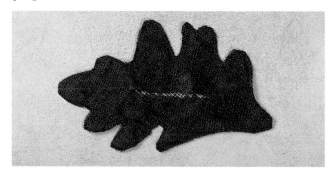

5. Gently turn the appliqué right side out, turning through the slit. Use a point turner in the narrow places.

6. Roll the seamline toward the underside (interfacing) and carefully press along the edges to adhere the rolled seamline in place. After the outer edges have been set, press the entire appliqué to adhere the interfacing. Pinch the slit together to eliminate wrinkles.

7. Lightly spray KK2000 on the wrong side of the interfaced appliqué and adhere in place.

8. Blindhem stitch appliqués in place, using the following guidelines:

a) For best visibility, use an open-toe appliqué foot or something comparable. (Do not use your machine's blindhem presser foot as that foot is designed to prevent dimpling on the catch stitch. To mimic hand stitching, you want the "dimple" as the stitch catches the appliqué.)

b) Use clear thread or regular thread in a color that won't be noticeable.

c) Experiment with the stitch width so you can secure an appropriate amount at the edge of the appliqué.

d) Adjust the stitch length to approximately 2mm for nice spacing between the catch stitches.

e) Since the blindhem stitch is designed for a completely different purpose, you may feel like you are sewing backwards when using it for appliqué. If you have a computerized sewing machine, engage the mirror image function and you will be able to position the fabric in the normal way.

Falling Leaves combines blindhem appliqué and echo stitching. Templates and directions are given on page 105.

Blanket Stitch Appliqué

This is the perfect choice for those times when you want a bold hand-stitched look. If the appliqué fabric doesn't ravel and offers a good blunt edge, this technique can be applied to the raw edge. If the appliqué fabric ravels, use lightweight fusible interfacing to turn under the raw edges (follow the directions given in blindhem appliqué).

1. Lightly spray KK2000 on the wrong side of the appliqué and adhere in place.
2. Blanket stitch the appliqué in place.
a) For best results, use a regular or appliqué presser foot that has a bar between the toes. This will keep the raw edge of the appliqué flat as it approaches the needle.
b) For a pretty blanket stitch, choose a contrast color rayon thread for the needle.
c) For a bolder blanket stitch, double up, using *two* strands of contrast color rayon thread. Thread your machine as you would for double needle stitching (refer to page 39 for directions) except run both threads through the eye of the single needle. When using two strands, use a needle one size larger to accommodate the extra thread bulk.
d) Set your machine for the blanket stitch (a ladder-looking stitch). If you have a computerized machine, try the mirror image setting to reverse the stitching direction. If you don't have a blanket stitch on your machine, experiment with similar style stitches such as the feather stitch.
e) Adjust the stitch width and length for a wide, bold stitch. Start out with the widest stitch width your machine allows and narrow the width until you have a depth you like. Then adjust the stitch length for a balanced look. Adjust the tension if necessary so the straight stitches lay nicely outside the outer edge of the appliqué.

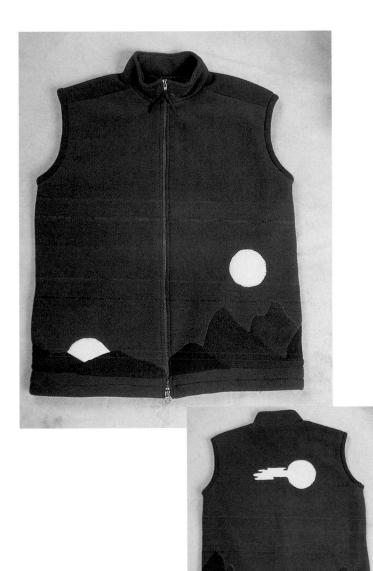

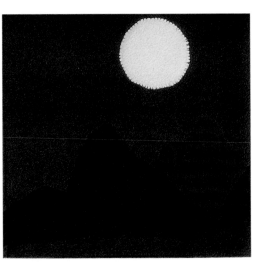

Nancy's Note

The larger and simpler the appliqué, the wider and bolder your blanket stitch can be. If your design is small, adjust your stitch to be proportionate yet still very noticeable.

Mountain Landscape is a wonderful blanket stitch appliqué that takes advantage of your fleece scrap stash. Since it makes such good use of leftovers, templates and directions are included in the Scrap Happy chapter.

Echo Stitching

When is an appliqué not an appliqué? When it is stitching only! While not really an appliqué, this stitching is a nice touch to incorporate with appliqués.

If you'd like to add more design detailing but fear that the addition of more appliqués would overwhelm or defeat the intended effect, try duplicating the motif by echo stitching only the appliqué outline, not the actual appliqué.

Good examples: tumbling leaves; a forest of trees; a spray of stars; an echo of hearts; a multi-layered mountain range; a flock of birds.

The outline stitching can be:
1. Blindhem or blanket stitch outlined (duplicating the look of the appliqué stitch).
2. Zigzag satin stitch sculptured (see the Sculpturing chapter).
3. Free-motion shadow stitched (see the Sculpturing chapter).
4. Double needle decorative stitch sculptured (see the Sculpturing chapter).
5. Double needle welt outlined (see the Pintucking chapter).

Experiment on a scrap of fleece to determine which stitch shows the best on the fabric you have chosen. If using a blanket stitch, feather stitch, or something comparable, consider using two strands of contrast rayon thread in a larger needle for a more noticeable effect.

If using a dense stitch for outline stitching (a zigzag satin stitch or equivalent), you will first need to stabilize the underside of the fleece with Totally Stable to prevent fabric distortion.

Determine how many actual appliqués you need. Then build the rest of the design by echo stitching a galaxy of stars or a flurry of leaves without the appliqués!

Heart Blanket – Blunt Edge Appliqué in Reverse

This blanket is designed for mid to heavier weight solid color fleece.

You Will Need

Lap blanket: 1 yard each of two contrast fleeces
Blanket: 1½ to 2 yards each of two contrast fleeces
Regular thread to match each color
Pattern tracing material
Sulky KK2000

Blanket Construction

1. Measure the length and width of the fleeces to plan for the number of motifs to be placed in each direction.
a) Allow for 1/2" seam allowance around all the edges.
b) Allow for 5" corner boxes (twice as large as border boxes).
c) Allow for 2½" border boxes.
d) Trim the length or width to match the motif box measurement needs.
2. Place the fleeces *wrong* sides together. Pin them together at a 90° angle to the cut edges.
3. With matching threads in the needle and bobbin (two different colors, matching each fleece color), sew a 1/2" seam allowance around the entire blanket.
4. Using a rotary cutter and ruler, trim to 1/4" away from the seamline on all sides.
5. Sew a 5" box in each corner.
6. Attach a quilt bar (spacer bar, edge guide, etc.) to your machine and sew one long 2½" border along the short edges and a long double 2½" border along the long edges.
7. Sew cross seams to form 2½" boxes in all borders.
8. On pattern tracing material, trace and cut out five to ten heart motifs.

Heart Template

9. Using the cutout heart motifs as a guide, lightly spray the heart with KK2000 and adhere it in a box. Stitch around the heart, then remove it. Spray again and stitch the next box. When the heart pattern gets too fuzzy, discard and use a new one.

10. Using appliqué or embroidery scissors, trim just the top layer to reveal the contrast underneath. Trim all the hearts on one side. (Only the outline stitching of the heart is visible on the opposing side.) Trim all the plain boxes on the other side. (Only the outlined stitching of the boxes is visible on the opposing side.) Results: Contrast hearts on one side of the blanket and contrast boxes on the other.

Optional Seam Finishes

Traditional: With right sides together, leaving an opening for turning. Turn, hand stitch, and top-stitch.

"Real" Blanket Stitching: Place the fleeces wrong sides together. For an easy gauge, topstitch at 1/2" to 5/8" in matching threads. Then hand blanket stitch, counting the machine seam stitches for an even gauge.

October Branches – Dimensional Appliqué With Sculpturing

Stark sculptured branches with a sprinkling of stubborn, curled dimensional autumn leaves refusing to drop to the ground.

1. Using the branches sketch on this page as a guide, sculpture stitch the branches on the garment.

a) Refer to the Sculpturing chapter for directions on how to transfer large designs. (*Note*: The branches sketch is already reversed for placement on the right shoulder.) Depending on the garment style and size chosen, extend the branches up to the shoulder or armscye and gracefully extend the branches across the garment front as desired. More branches may be added.

b) The garment center front line is given as a suggested guideline only. Place branches as desired.

c) Sculpture satin stitch, varying the branch widths from thicker (toward the shoulder) to spindly (toward the branch ends).

2. Remove the Totally Stable stabilizer and discard.

3. Use the leaf templates to cut out as many leaves as desired.

4. Stitch and attach as many leaves as desired, following the dimensional appliqué directions on page 98.

5. Launder the garment inside out using the machine's gentle cycle.

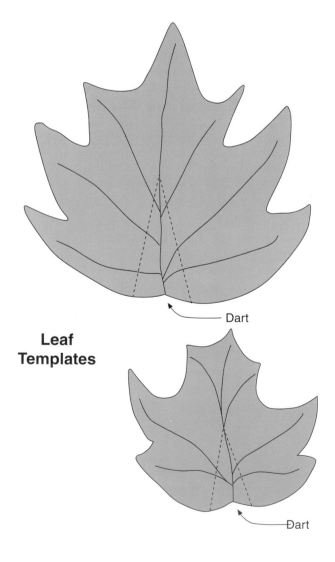

Leaf Templates

Dart

Dart

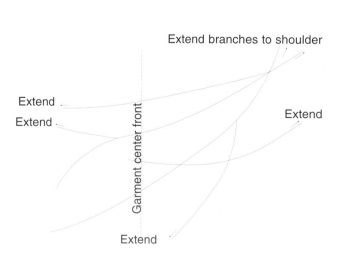

Extend branches to shoulder

Extend

Extend

Extend

Garment center front

Extend

Falling Leaves - Blindhem Appliqué With Echo Stitching

A flurry of blindhem appliquéd plaid flannel leaves and echo-stitched leaves tumbling from one shoulder, across the front toward the lower opposite hemline.

1. Cut an assortment of Large Leaf #1, Large Leaf #2, Leaf #3, and Leaf #4 from a small plaid flannel. Use Medium Leaf #1 and #2 for detail stitching, satin stitching, blunt edge appliqué, or echo stitching accents.

2. Sew the plaid leaf motifs to fusible interfacing and turn to the finished position, following the blindhem appliqué directions on pages 99-100.

3. Arrange the leaves on the garment front, graduating from larger to smaller or smaller to larger, depending on your taste.

4. Echo stitch as many leaves as necessary to create an autumn flurry. Echo stitch with the blindhem stitch, blanket stitch, or another comparable hand-stitched look stitch. If desired, use two strands of thread and adjust the stitch length and width to be more noticeable.

Falling Leaves Templates

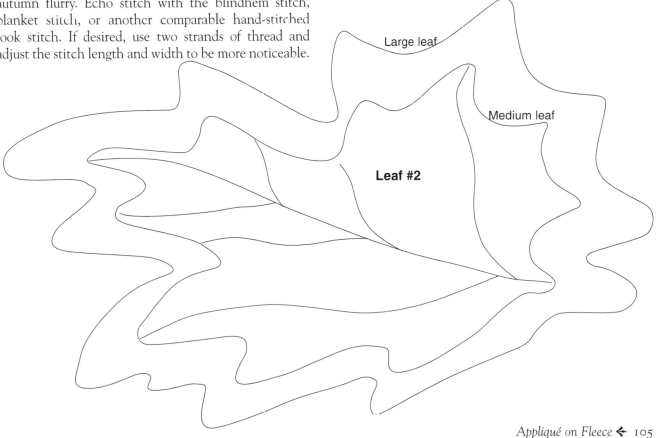

Large leaf

Medium leaf

Leaf #2

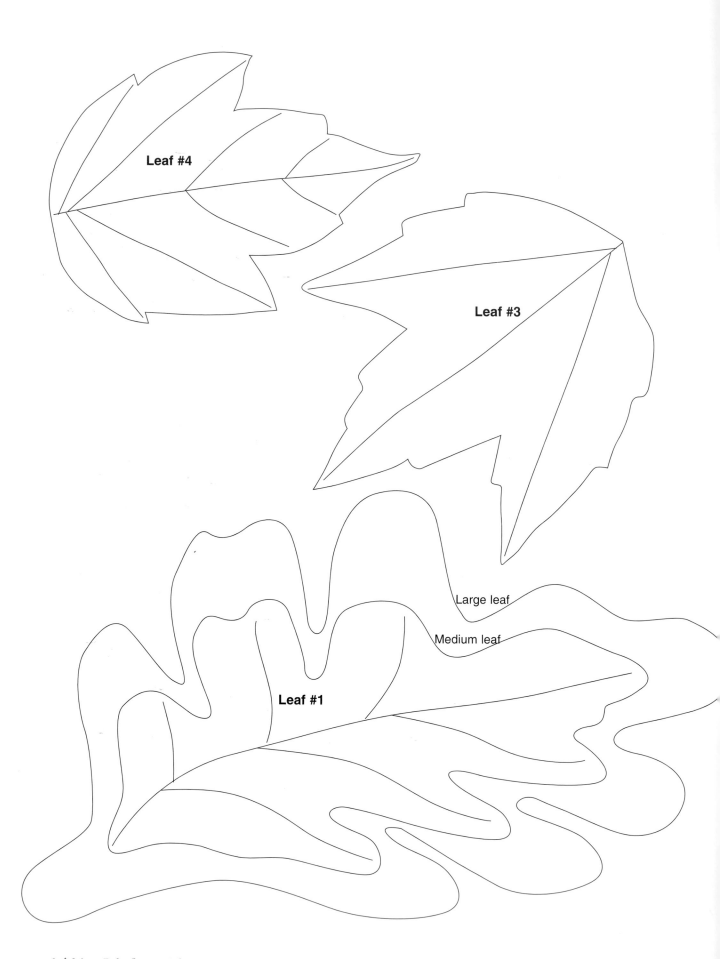

Leaf #4

Leaf #3

Large leaf

Medium leaf

Leaf #1

Mountain Scene Landscape – Blanket Stitch Appliqué

This show-stopper landscape appliqué is not only fun and easy to build, but it helps you clean out your scrap stash of leftover fleece pieces! Theoretically, the directions and templates belong in this chapter because the mountains, sun, moon, and clouds are blanket stitch appliquéd in place. However, this scene makes such tremendous use of leftover scraps and pieces that the templates and directions are included in the last chapter, Scrap Happy (see page 134).

Creating the landscape is easy. You'll spend more time and effort deciding on the color combinations!

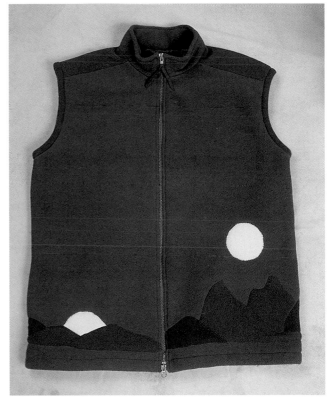

Chapter 7

BUTTONHOLES & SPORT SNAPS

Zippers and sport snaps are frequently used as closures on fleece garments, but there are many times when only a buttonhole will do. A good old basic buttonhole, or perhaps one that offers a designer accent. Buttonholes on fleece aren't difficult, they just require a slightly different approach than the everyday standard buttonhole.

The purpose of a buttonhole on woven fabrics is to stabilize and prevent the slit opening from raveling. Fleece is a knit and doesn't ravel, so you don't need the buttonhole stitching to prevent raveling. But the buttonhole area still needs to be stabilized.

First, here's a review of the basic buttonhole procedures as presented in *Adventures With Polarfleece*. Although I only refer to fleece, the process is the same for fleece, Berber, and plush fabrics. After the basics, we'll explore a few variations.

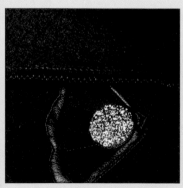

Doris Zopfi loves the warmth of fleece but wanted something a bit dressier. So she sculptured subtle tone-on-tone fan motifs on the collar and cuffs. (Using the small motif transfer technique in Chapter 2 on page 33.) Again using the fan design, she layered UltraSuede and UltraLeather to create the buttonholes using the UltraSuede Cheater's Buttonhole (page 116).

Basic Buttonholes on Fleece

The Rules & The Reasoning

Nancy's Tip

Always, always, always do a sample buttonhole first! On a scrap of fleece, sew test buttonholes using the ***same lengthwise or crossgrain*** *as the real buttonholes will be. Make the test conditions identical to the real conditions.*

Following the directions below, use the test sample to fine tune the buttonhole for look and length. Better safe than sorry. Personally, tearing out unacceptable buttonholes is not my idea of fun!

Fleece Buttonholes

1. Draw the buttonhole markings on Solvy. Because fleece is a fuzzy fabric, it is difficult to draw an accurate buttonhole length directly on the fleece itself. Use a permanent marker, wash-out marker, or a disappearing ink marker to draw the buttonholes on the Solvy. Drawing the buttonhole on Solvy serves many useful purposes:

a) It gives an accurate drawn length to stitch.

b) It acts as a stabilizer and prevents stretching.

c) It acts as a topping and helps keep the buttonhole stitches laying on top of the fleece rather than sinking deeply into the loft of the fabric.

2. Insert interfacing behind the buttonhole if possible. If the buttonhole area offers two layers of fleece on which to sew the buttonhole (the garment has a facing layer or is lined), insert a piece of woven interfacing between the layers in the buttonhole area. Fleece has enough body on its own and rarely needs interfacing for the entire garment front edge, but interfacing in both the buttonhole and the button sew-on area insures strength. (If your garment is a single layer of fabric, many buttonhole options are offered in this chapter, along with using sport snaps.)

3. Attach the drawn Solvy to the buttonhole placement markings. Pin or adhere (the easiest method) in place. If adhering, lightly spray Sulky KK2000 temporary adhesive on the wrong side of the drawn Solvy and adhere it in place.

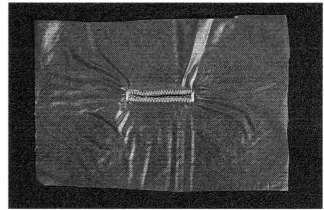

4. Alter your sewing machine's preset buttonhole settings. Lengthen the stitch length so you can see a hint of fabric between the zigzag stitches. Loosen up. Remember that the original purpose of a tight satin stitch buttonhole is to inhibit raveling. Since fleece doesn't ravel, you don't need "inhibited" buttonholes. A too-dense, too-tight satin stitch buttonhole results in the dreaded frog-mouth buttonhole.

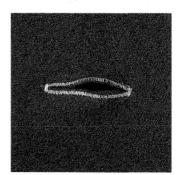

The dreaded frog-mouth buttonhole.

Because fleece is a knit with stretch, the buttonhole cut edge will react if too much thread is piled in. As soon as the buttonhole opening is cut, too-dense buttonhole edges will ripple, or frog mouth. Loosening up eliminates this potential problem.

5. Loosen the needle tension for the buttonhole setting if necessary. In regular buttonholes, you want the needle thread to pull slightly to the underside, resulting in a smooth upper stitch. With the loft of fleece, it is quite likely that the knot of the bobbin in the stitch formation will not be visible. You may not even have to change the needle tension. A sample buttonhole will determine if the needle tension needs to be adjusted.

6. Sew the buttonhole.

7. Remove the excess drawn Solvy. Any visible Solvy remaining in the stitches will be removed in the first laundering.

Nancy's Hint

So many sewing techniques are just common sense; sewing fleece buttonholes is another one of those common sense procedures.

*If the buttonhole is horizontal (which most are), sew it so the presser foot is **always** in complete contact with fabric. (Sounds obvious, but we don't always do the obvious thing.) This tip applies to all buttonholes, not just fleece.*

You have the choice of sewing your buttonhole in one of two directions:

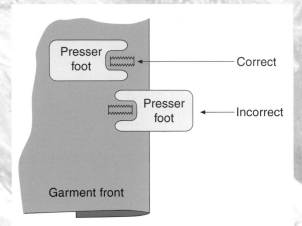

#1. From the garment body toward the center front edge (which keeps the presser foot in total contact with the fabric at all times).

Or...

#2. From the center front edge toward the garment body (which positions the presser foot so the back end hangs off the center front edge part of the time).

You have better feed control and more consistent stitching when you have continual and total contact between the presser foot, fabric, and feed dogs. Choose #1 and sew from the body toward the center front edge.

Self-Fabric "Interfaced" Buttonhole

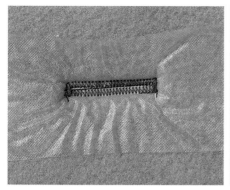  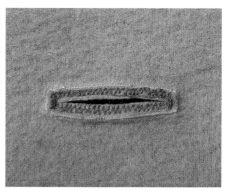

This too-good-to-be-true buttonhole was first featured in *Adventures With Polarfleece*. It is the perfect solution for simple buttonholes made on a single layer of fleece. Since there is no place to insert real interfacing to support the buttonhole, self fabric is used to interface the buttonhole. (Not suitable for Berber or plush fabrics.)

1. Per the directions for a basic buttonhole, draw the buttonhole on Solvy and adhere it to the right side of the garment.

2. With wrong sides together, place a patch of self fabric fleece behind each buttonhole area. No need to be too particular about the shape or size because the patch will be cut away when finished.

3. Place the patch so the greater degree of stretch in the patch is opposite the greater degree of stretch in the garment.

4. Sew the buttonhole, following the directions for basic buttonholes on pages 109-110.

5. Use sharp scissors to trim the patch away, trimming very close to the buttonhole stitching. This results in a double layer of fabric in the buttonhole area and gives a nice amount of stabilization. Because you used self fabric, the color match is perfect!

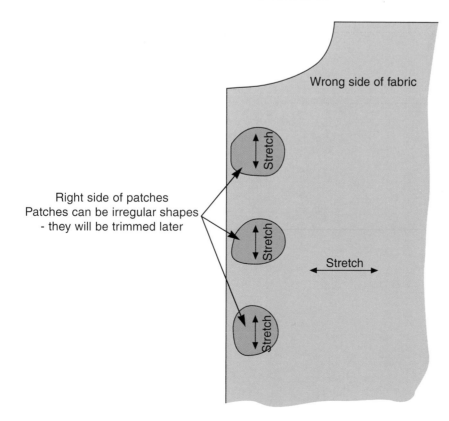

Wrong side of fabric

Right side of patches
Patches can be irregular shapes
- they will be trimmed later

Stretch

$\mathcal{F}$leece Welt Buttonhole

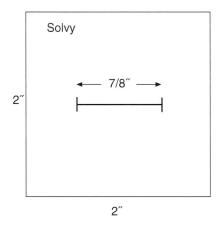

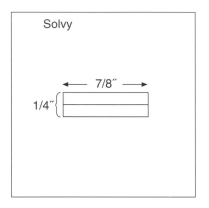

Here's another great buttonhole option for *single layer* garments. This one works best when buttons are 3/4" or larger in diameter. If using a heavyweight fleece, use a 1" or larger button. As always, do a test buttonhole on a scrap of fleece! The example illustrated here is for a 3/4" button. (Not suitable for Berber or plush fabrics.)

1. On a 2" square piece of Solvy, use a permanent marker or wash-out marker to draw the buttonhole length. The buttonhole length is the button diameter plus the height of the button, which is usually 1/8" (3/4" + 1/8" = 7/8").

2. Draw a rectangle for the welt opening, 1/8" either side of the drawn buttonhole length and the exact length of the buttonhole line. (Double check: the resulting welt opening should be 1/4" wide x the buttonhole length.)

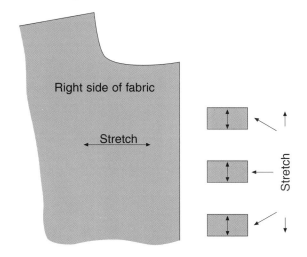

3. Cut a fleece patch 2" high x at least 2" longer than the button diameter (in this example, 2" x 2¾"). Have the greater degree of stretch in the height (opposite the direction of the buttonhole).
4. Lightly spray the drawn Solvy with Sulky KK2000 and adhere to the *wrong* side of a fleece patch.
5. Mark the buttonhole placements on the garment according to the pattern directions.
6. With right sides together, pin the Solvy/fleece patch to the garment at the buttonhole placement marking. (Double check: the fleece patch is on the right side of the garment with the drawn Solvy on top.)

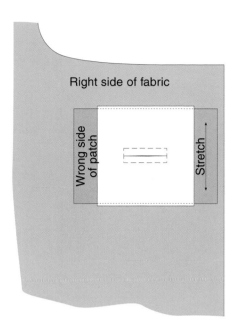

Right side of fabric

Wrong side of patch

Stretch

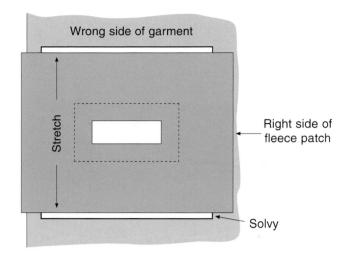

Wrong side of garment

Stretch

Right side of fleece patch

Solvy

7. Using a 2.5 to 3mm stitch length and beginning on one long side of the drawn rectangle, straight stitch around the buttonhole, overlapping at the beginning and ending stitches.

10. Gently turn the welt patch to the wrong side of the garment and finger press to lay flat.

11. Topstitch at 1/4" around the welt opening.

Nancy's Hint

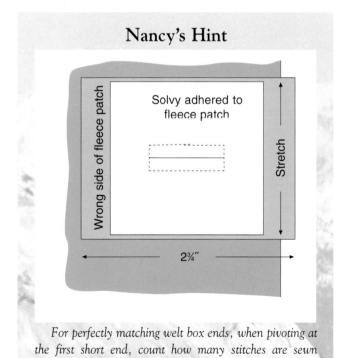

Wrong side of fleece patch

Solvy adhered to fleece patch

Stretch

2¾"

For perfectly matching welt box ends, when pivoting at the first short end, count how many stitches are sewn between the corners. Stitch the same number of stitches when sewing the other end of the box. A perfect match!

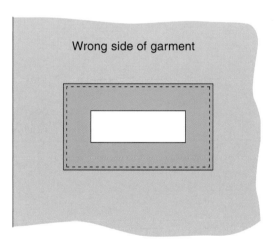

Wrong side of garment

12. From the wrong side, trim the excess patch close to the topstitching.

8. Remove the Solvy.

9. Very carefully cut the buttonhole opening. Be careful not to cut through the stitching lines at the end of box.

UltraSuede Backwards Welt Buttonhole

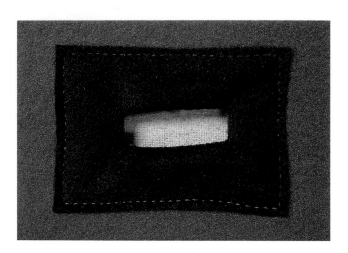

The welt opening is similar to the fleece welt buttonhole except that the UltraSuede patch is stitched to the *wrong* side of the garment. When the patch is turned to the finished position, the UltraSuede patch becomes an accent on the right side of the garment, leaving a completely finished wrong side! Great for *single layer* fleece, Berber, and plush garments. The example illustrated here is for a 3/4" button.

1. For each buttonhole, cut an UltraSuede patch in the desired size and shape. The minimum recommended size is 1/2" larger than the button diameter (1" larger is stronger, easier to handle, and looks nicer. Make a test buttonhole to determine which size looks best on your garment). A 3/4" button requires a patch at least 1¼" high x 1¼" long. Patches may be irregular in size and shape as long as they are larger than the minimums. Rectangular patches are classic.

2. Because UltraSuede has little stretch and is easy to mark, draw the buttonhole length directly on the wrong side of the UltraSuede patch. The buttonhole length is the button diameter plus the height of the button, which is usually 1/8" (3/4" + 1/8" = 7/8").

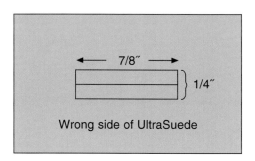

Wrong side of UltraSuede

3. Draw a rectangle for the welt opening, 1/8" either side of the drawn buttonhole length and the exact length of the buttonhole line. (Double check: the resulting welt opening should be 1/4" wide x the buttonhole length.)

4. Mark the buttonhole placements on the garment according to the pattern directions.

5. Place the *right side* of the UltraSuede patch against the *wrong side* of the fleece at the buttonhole placement markings. Tape in place if necessary, but don't pin or adhere in place.

6. Using a 2.5 to 3mm stitch length and beginning on one long side of the drawn rectangle, straight stitch around the buttonhole, overlapping the beginning and ending stitches.

Nancy's Hint

For perfectly matched welt box ends, when pivoting at the first short end, count how many stitches are taken between corners. Stitch the same number of stitches when sewing the other end of the box.

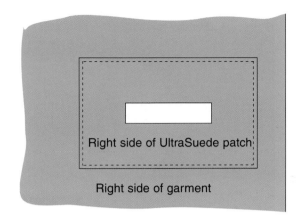

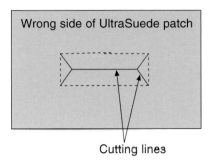

Cutting lines

7. Use small sharp scissors to very carefully cut the buttonhole opening. For ease in turning the UltraSuede, cut into the corners of the welt opening, creating a wedge, being careful not to cut through the stitches.

8. Gently turn the UltraSuede patch to the right side of the garment and finger press it to lay flat.

Nancy's Hint

To get nicely squared edges at the ends of the welt opening, grab both short ends of the patch and give a gentle tug.

9. Edgestitch the UltraSuede patch to the garment to secure. Edgestitch around the buttonhole opening if needed.

Nancy's Hint

An edgestitch presser foot makes this step quick, easy, and accurate!

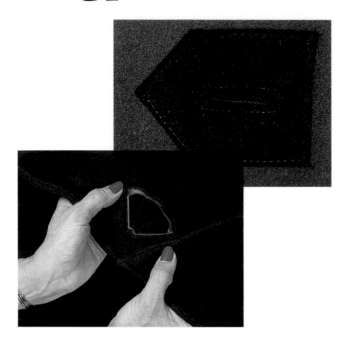

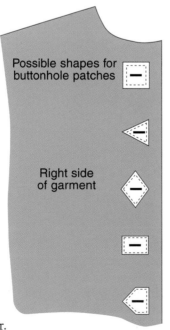

Since neither fleece nor UltraSuede ravel, take advantage of both for a quick and simple topstitched box with a slit opening for a buttonhole. Great for *single or double layer* garments made from fleece, Berber, or plush fabrics. It's called cheater's because you simply stitch a box and cut a slit opening for the button. What could be easier?

Decide whether you want a round, square, rectangular, or irregular shaped UltraSuede buttonhole patch. The patch can be any shape and size that is complementary to your garment. (Place your button on a piece of paper and experiment with patch shapes and sizes.) The minimum recommended size is 1/2" larger than the button diameter (1" larger is stronger, easier to handle, and looks nicer.

Possible shapes for buttonhole patches

Right side of garment

Make a test buttonhole to determine which size looks best). A 3/4" button requires a patch at least 1¼" high x 1¼" long.

Nancy's Caution

Remember that even though the buttonhole is centered in the patch, when the garment is on your body, the button will pull to one side of the buttonhole. This may make your button appear off center on a smaller symmetrical shape like a square or round patch. Make a test buttonhole and adjust the size or shape if necessary for the look you want.

1. Using a Chacopel pencil, draw a horizontal line on the right side of the UltraSuede patch for the buttonhole opening. The buttonhole length is the button diameter plus the height of the button, which is usually 1/8".

2. Mark the buttonhole placements per the pattern directions.

3. Lightly spray the wrong side of the UltraSuede patch with Sulky KK2000. Adhere the UltraSuede patch to the right side of the garment at the buttonhole markings.

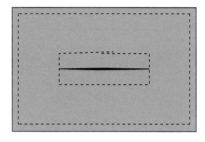

4. Using a 3mm straight stitch, edgestitch the patch to the garment at 1/8".

5. Using a 2.5mm straight stitch, sew a rectangle 1/8" away from the drawn buttonhole line, stitching the short ends exactly at the ends of the drawn buttonhole line. Begin and end on one long side, overlapping a few stitches when ending.

6. Carefully cut the buttonhole open.

Sport Snaps & Polarfleece

A Winning Combination!

Sport snaps offer a terrific alternative to button and zipper closures. Long-prong size 20 and 24 are the preferred style and sizes for fleece garments. These sizes easily grasp and securely hold two layers of 200 weight (mid-weight) fleece.

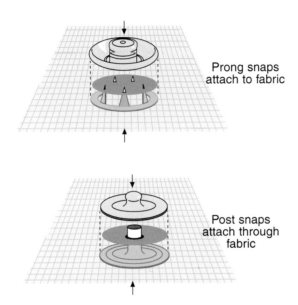

Prong snaps attach to fabric

Post snaps attach through fabric

Because fleece, Berber, and plush fabrics are knitted, prong-style snaps bite into and grab the fleece, evenly anchoring the perimeter of the snap. Post-style snaps, better suited for woven fabrics, require a hole to be punched in the fabric to accommodate the snap. The punched hole on a knitted fabric will stretch, resulting in the snap pulling away from the fabric. Use the post-style snap only if it is to be attached to woven trim.

When purchasing sport snaps for use on fleece, carefully check the prong length. I recommend Snap Source snaps because they offer one of the longest pronged snaps on the market. The longer the prong length, the better the grip and the stronger the hold.

The following "Polar Snap Tips" were provided by and reprinted with permission of Jeanine Twigg, the acknowledged industry snap expert and founder of The Snap Source, Inc. Her book, *It's A Snap!*, is an encyclopedia of snap information, technique, and usage ideas.

Polar Snap Tips
Stabilizing Ideas

1. If the garment offers two layers of fleece, insert a piece of woven interfacing between the layers in the snap area.

2. If two layers of fleece are too bulky, replace the fleece facing, under collar, or inner cuff with two layers of a complementary woven fabric. This will both reduce bulk and act as a stabilizer for the snaps. (This is the perfect solution for snapped front garments where four layers of fleece in the lapped area would be too bulky.) Understitching the seam allowance to the woven maintains an even seam edge and prevents unwanted "peeking out" of the inside layers.

3. On a single-layer garment, cut an UltraSuede patch and edgestitch it in place. Apply sport snaps on the UltraSuede patch. (If you don't want an accent patch on the right side of the garment, place the UltraSuede patch on the inside of the garment.)

Fabric Compression
Or... X Marks the Spot!

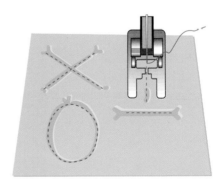

When attaching snaps to fleece and pile fabrics, another bulk-reducing technique is to compress the fabric before setting the snap. To compress the fabric, use your sewing machine to stitch an X, O, or + over each snap placement mark, compacting that area. Stitch the compression smaller than the snap size and you don't even have to remove the stitching!

For a terrific selection of alternative buttonhole treatments, refer to *Adventures With Polarfleece* where you'll find a variety of UltraSuede buttonhole loops, patches, tabs, and sport snap applications.

Chapter 8

FINISHING TOUCHES

The marks of a designer garment are often found in the little things. Attention to small details that lend an air of distinction. These small details aren't difficult, they are simply little extras that add appeal (and dollar value) to the price tag. This is where the imaginative and creative home sewer has a distinct advantage!

In this chapter, you'll find easy ways to dress up boring zippers, embellish plain garments with decoratively stitched ribbon, add a variety of edge finishes, and even create fleece rickrack trim!

Stylish Zipper Treatments

Since fleece garments today are commonly worn as indoor wear, replacing sweatshirts and sweaters, you will find that many ready-made garments and sewing patterns eliminate the facings that traditionally sandwiched the zipper, hiding the raw zipper tape. The elimination of the facings is most frequently seen in zippered pullovers and lighter jackets. It is nice for reducing bulk, but when the collar is worn unzipped and open, the resulting "naked" zipper tape looks unsightly, to say the least. Here are two quick and easy designer finishes to add a touch of class to those garments.

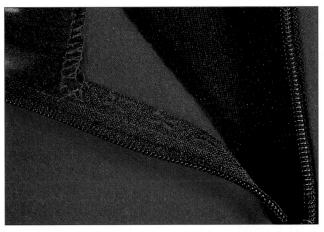

Embellished Zipper Tape

This quick and easy idea involves nothing more than sewing a pretty decorative sewing machine stitch on the zipper tape *before* applying it to your garment. There is no change to the method of zipper application or any changes to the garment. Just a little beautification to an otherwise boring zipper tape!

1. Place rayon thread in an embroidery needle and regular thread in the bobbin. (The thread can match or contrast the zipper color, the fleece color, or accent a color in the print.)
2. Loosen the needle tension a little so the upper stitches pull slightly to the underside.
3. Choose a simple satin stitch design on your machine.
a) Choose a stitch with some fill-in qualities so it will be visible. Delicate open designs will not be showy enough to complement the garment.
b) Choose a decorative stitch 5mm or narrower in width or one that can be narrowed to that width. Since you will be stitching directly on the zipper tape, you have a restricted area that cannot accommodate large dramatic designs.
4. Using an appliqué presser foot, slip the zipper tape *wrong* side up under the presser foot. To keep the stitches from puckering, slip a piece of tear-away stabilizer under the zipper tape.

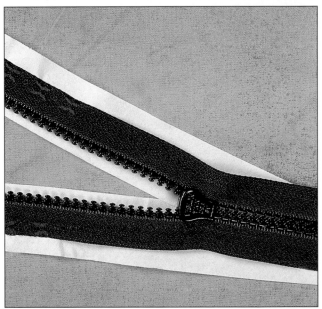

Nancy's Caution

*Make sure you have the zipper tape **wrong** side up. It feels very wrong to be embellishing on the wrong side of something, but when a zippered collar or front is worn open, it's the wrong side of the zipper tape that will be visible. So that's the side to dress up.*

5. Guide the zipper tape so the edge of the presser foot grazes alongside the zipper teeth. (There isn't a lot of room to work here, so sew slowly and carefully guide the zipper tape.)

6. To align the designs so they match on both sides of the zipper tape (it's always a nice touch when the motifs match up!), chalk mark a beginning spot above the bottom zipper stop. Sew from the bottom of the zipper tape up to the top. On both sides, make sure to begin stitching with the first stitch of your motif. (If you have a computerized machine, engage the pattern begin function. If you have a mechanical machine, refer to the machine manual to get to the beginning of a motif.) When stitching the second side, you may have to push or pull a little to keep the motifs exactly lined up.

7. Remove the stabilizer.

8. Apply the zipper to the garment in the usual manner, following the pattern directions.

Dressing a Naked Zipper

First featured in *Adventures With Polarfleece*, this technique is another way to dress up the raw edge of visible zipper tape. This technique is featured in better sportswear fleece garments. When the neckline is worn open, the little bit of color trim wrapping the edges of the zipper tape looks classy and finished. Like the embellished zipper tape on page 119, this technique is done to the zipper *before* application to the garment and does not change the garment construction steps.

1. Purchase 5/8" grosgrain ribbon two times longer than your zipper, plus a couple inches of "grace room." Choose a ribbon color to complement your garment. It can match or contrast. Ready-to-wear companies frequently choose a completely different color from any featured in the garment, which basically says, "Anything goes!"

Nancy's Caution

Be careful when choosing ribbon trim for your garment. Many ribbons on the market are aimed at craft usage and not intended to be sewn into garments. Make sure the ribbon is 100% polyester and washable. I chose grosgrain ribbon because it is easily found at both fabric and craft stores. However, any colorfast washable trim with finished edges on both edges will work.

2. Press the ribbon in half lengthwise. *Note*: Polyester ribbons tend to be springy and not excited about being pressed in half. However, with extra steam, pressure, and time you will win the battle of wills. I like to press and pin my ribbon to the ironing boarding until it cools. If you have an exceptionally stubborn piece of trim, use wash-away basting tape to adhere the ribbon trim to the zipper tape.

3. Slip the folded ribbon over each long edge of the zipper tape, encasing the edges. Edgestitch in place. For easy and accurate ribbon application, use an edgestitch presser foot and move the needle position over as much as necessary to catch both the upper and under edges of the ribbon.

4. Sew the zipper to the garment according to the pattern directions.

Embellished Grosgrain Ribbon Trim

Play with the decorative stitches on your machine to embellish grosgrain ribbon. Then use the decorated trim to enliven an ordinary garment. Depending on your fabric and stitch choice, you can achieve an alpine look, pull out a motif to accent a fleece print, or simply dress up a solid color garment.

For the adventuresome sewer, use a double needle to embellish with decorative stitches from your machine. Refer to double needle sculpturing on page 24-26 for information on how to set up your machine.

Decoratively stitch the ribbon and edgestitch it in place to secure to the garment. Use the embellished ribbon to cover shoulder seams, frame a zipper, frame a welt pocket, cover a yoke seamline, or to create a decorative lattice on a plain garment front. You can also apply embellished ribbon trim along the hem, cuff, or hood edges. Add as much or as little as suits your taste and style.

For a clever way to hide zipper seam allowances, refer to the "backwards" zipper in *Adventures With Polarfleece*. There are no visible seam allowances inside or out!

Nancy's Hint

If you have a yoke or pocket seam that isn't quite up to your standards, it's much more fun to cover it with embellished ribbon than it is to tear it out and re-sew! (We are in this for fun, aren't we?)

You Will Need

→ 5/8" grosgrain ribbon - measure all the edges and seamlines you want to cover and add an extra yard or two to allow plenty for experimental sample stitching as well as design changes (sewers are known for changing horses in midstream)

→ Decorative thread - for embellishing stitches on trim

→ Embroidery or metallic needle - whichever is appropriate for your chosen thread

→ 1 to 2 yards tear-away stabilizer

→ Wash-A-Way Wonder Tape

Nancy's Note

High quality, 100% polyester grosgrain ribbon does not shrink or bleed excess color. If in doubt about the quality of your ribbon, pretreat it in a bowl of warm sudsy water. If the water discolors, rinse the ribbon and soak it in white vinegar and water or a color retaining product to help set the color. Place the ribbon in a laundry bag or pillowcase and toss in the dryer.

1. Place decorative thread in the appropriate needle and regular thread in the bobbin. Loosen the needle tension so the stitches pull slightly to the underside.

2. Cut tear-away stabilizer into approximately 1" strips and slip the strips under the ribbon to stabilize while stitching.

3. Choose a decorative stitch or sequence of stitches on the machine and test sew a sample, adjusting the stitch width and density as needed. For best visibility and accent potential, choose stitches with fill-in satin stitch areas. Your test sample is a good place to experiment with a variety of stitches.

4. Decorative stitch the entire length of the ribbon. When stitching, continue adding stabilizer strips as necessary.

5. Tear away the stabilizer and discard.

6. Press the ribbon flat.

7. Edgestitch the ribbon to the garment as desired. Plan first, sew second. Plan the placement of the embellished ribbon so the ribbon ends will be caught in the seamlines rather than having to be turned under for finishing.

For example:

a) Sew the front to the back at the shoulder seams .

b) Edgestitch the embellished ribbon in place, covering the shoulder seams.

c) Attach the collar and sleeves, catching the raw ends of the ribbon in the seams.

❧ Edge Finishes ❧

Quick-As-a-Wink Rotary Edge Finish

One of the nicest aspects of sewing with fleece is that there are so many places you can "cheat" and get away with it. Because fleece doesn't ravel, you can take advantage of this characteristic to save time and get great effects at the same time.

If your fleece is a better quality medium weight dense fleece that leaves a clean blunt edge when cut with a rotary cutter, you can use this feature to your benefit.

On collars and cuffs, instead of sewing in the traditional manner (right sides together and turning), you can eliminate all the bulk from the seam allowances by sewing *wrong* sides together, then rotary trimming along the stitching line, and leaving the edges raw! *Note:* You are stitching first, trimming second.

On patch pockets, instead of fighting bulky pocket seam allowances and trying to match corners, simply use wash-away basting tape to adhere pockets in place, leaving the raw edges exposed! Topstitch in place. No bulk. Even corners. Couldn't be easier!

Going a step further, let's have some fun with fleece raw edges. Insert a wavy edge rotary blade and you'll love the decorative edges. Not just practical, but very pretty too!

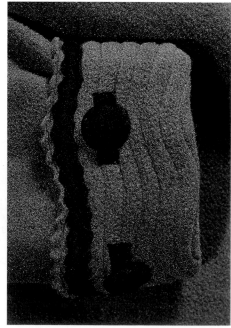

Ideas of How and Where to Use:

Royal Wavy Edge Shawl Collar Jacket

One simple change eliminated the bulk and added the bonus of a fancy wavy-edged finish to this shawl collar jacket. Instead of sewing the shawl collar to the collar facings right-sides-together, trimming, and turning (the usual construction method), I used a conventional sewing machine and sewed the shawl collar to the facing *wrong sides together*. I still used the 5/8" seam allowance as directed by the pattern, but the seam allowance ended up on the outside (visible side) of the jacket.

Using the wavy rotary blade, I then trimmed off the exposed seam allowance, approximately 1/4" away from the seamline. Pretty. Feminine. Easy. And no bulk! Looks hard but the rotary blade did all the work!

Purple Swing Coat

Instead of turning under and topstitching the scarf and coat edges, the wavy rotary blade gives an eye-catching finish in a fraction of the time! For instructions on how to do the additional embellishments of sculpturing and embroidery, refer to those chapters in this book.

Kid Outfit

Print + Solid + Wavy Rotary Blade = FUN!

Pati Sutton had fun combining three fleece embellishment techniques: a sculptured rose on the center back (see Chapter 2, pages 33-34 for large design transfer instructions); subtle tone-on tone meandering sculpturing down the front and on the cuffs; and easy and quick wavy edge rotary cut edges.

Wavy-edged lapped seams. Wavy piping inserted in pant leg seams. Wavy-edged mittens made from scraps. Quick to make and fun to wear. (See the Scrap Happy chapter for mitten directions.)

Fleece Rickrack

What do you get when you cut narrow strips of fleece with a rotary cutter? Fleece rickrack trim!

Thanks go to Julie Muschamp for this wonderful and easy embellishment idea.

1. Using your wavy edge rotary blade, cut 3/8" to 1/2" strips of fleece on the straight or crossgrain.

2. Use the fleece rickrack as decorative trim to cover seamlines, outline motifs, or make freeform designs.

3. Use wash-away basting tape to hold the fleece rickrack in place for stitching if necessary.

4. Stitch the rickrack to the garment using 3.0 or 4.0 double needles, or edgestitch along both sides.

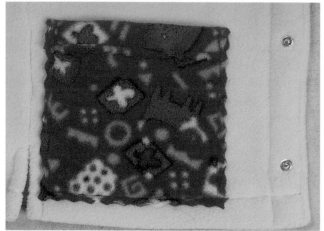

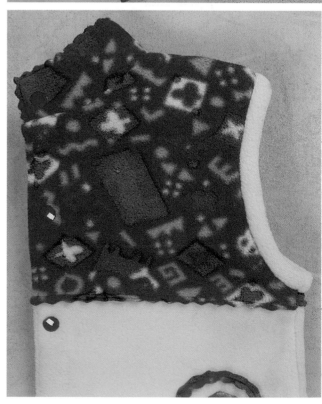

Quick Fringe Finish

Introduced in *Adventures With Polarfleece*, this technique is a super-fast way to fringe the edges of a blanket, pillow, vest, scarf, or hat. Use this technique when making the Quick Fringe Hat or Scarf in the Scrap Happy chapter.

You Will Need

→ 1 large cutting mat
→ 1 small cutting mat
→ Rotary cutter

1. Lay the fleece on the larger cutting mat.
2. Lay a small cutting mat on the fleece, 3" (or whatever depth you want the fringe to be) from the end of the fleece to be fringed.
3. Fold the fleece to be fringed over the small mat.

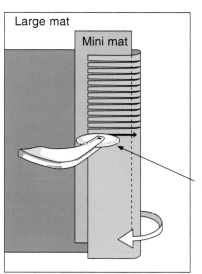

Fold over desired fringe depth

4. Use a rotary cutter to cut 1/2" fringe. Cut from the small mat and "run" onto the large mat.

Scalloped Edge Finish

Although you generally find this delicate scalloped edge technique on lingerie items and interlock knit tops, it also works beautifully on fleece. Perfect for those times when subtlety is desired.

1. Place regular thread in the needle and bobbin. Choose a thread color to match the fabric.

2. Select the blindhem stitch on your machine but use the all-purpose zigzag presser foot. The blindhem stitch sews a series of straight stitches then swings with one zigzag stitch to the left before sewing another series of straight stitches.

a) Turn under 3/8" along the edge to be scalloped.

b) With the *wrong* side up, place the folded edge of the fabric so the straight stitch is on the fleece hem and the one zigzag stitch swings over and completely off the fold of the fabric.

c) Sew a few test stitches on a scrap to test the stitch length, width, and needle tension. The stitch length determines the length of the scallop, the stitch width determines how deep the scallop can be, and the needle tension determines how much the fleece will draw in to create the scallop. Tighten the needle tension, if necessary, until you have the desired scallop.

d) Be careful not to stretch the fleece when sewing on the crossgrain.

Nancy's Note

Why this works…

If you were doing a real blindhem, you would attach the blindhem presser foot. When sewing, the zigzag portion of the stitch would swing from the hem allowance onto the base of your garment. The blindhem foot is designed with a center blade that builds in extra thread ease to prevent stitch dimples in your blindhem.

By using a regular presser foot, the zigzag stitch is tighter than with the blindhem presser foot. Then you allow the swing of the zigzag stitch to go completely over the edge of the raw fabric into "nothingness." Since the bobbin is knotting every stitch and there is no fabric to hold the stitch, the bobbin pulls the needle thread tighter. All these factors cause the edge of the fabric to pull in and scallop. In essence, you are sewing incorrectly for a purpose!

3. Since the capabilities of machines vary widely, sew a test sample to set up your machine for the best results.
If you have an older machine:

a) Set the stitch width as wide as it will go, probably 4mm to 5mm.

b) Adjust the stitch length to give you about 1/4" between zigzag stitches, or longer if you want longer scallops.

c) Since the straight stitches are on the right and the zigzag swings to the left, position your fabric so the bulk of the fleece is to the right of the needle (toward the body of your machine) and the folded edge is to the left of the needle (under the presser foot). This feels like you are sewing backwards.

If you have a newer computerized machine:

a) Set the stitch width anywhere from 5mm to 7mm wide. (You can experiment even wider to see if you like the look.)

b) Adjust the stitch length until you have a nice scalloped effect for the stitch width you are using.

c) Engage the mirror image function. This will reverse the blindhem stitch so the straight stitches are on the left and the zigzag swing is to the right. This allows you to place the fabric under the presser foot and sew the way you normally do.

4. Trim the fleece hem allowance close to the stitching.

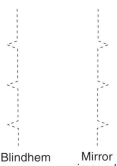

Blindhem   Mirror imaged

Close-up edge of garment

Blanket Stitching

A blanket stitch edge finish is a nice folksy touch that can be applied to vest edges, shawl collars, pockets, cuffs, hat bands, appliqués, and blankets. Blanket stitches can be sewn on raw edges or added to traditional seamed edges. You can use yarn to blanket stitch by hand or take advantage of your computerized machine with larger stitch capabilities and blanket stitch by machine. Or you can "cheat" and do a mock blanket stitch on your serger!

Raw Edge Hand Blanket Stitch

Enjoy hand finishing the raw fleece edges while taking advantage of your sewing machine to get perfectly spaced blanket stitches. For an easy way to get even and consistent blanket stitches, use a contrast basting stitch on your sewing-machine and sew a "stitch gauge" alongside the raw edge. As you hand stitch, simply count the basting stitches to know where to take your next stitch!

With contrast color thread in the needle, machine baste a stitch gauge as follows:

1. Determine how deep you want the blanket stitches. Sew the basting stitches this depth away from the raw edge (3/8" offers a nice understated look, 5/8" is bolder).

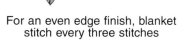

For an even edge finish, blanket stitch every three stitches

2. Determine how far apart you want the blanket stitches to be. Choose 3/8" to 5/8" spacing to balance the chosen depth.

3. On a test sample of fleece, experiment with the stitch length so you can stitch the ladder rungs of the blanket stitch every three or four basting stitches. (The longer the basting stitches, the easier they are to remove.)

4. Using a tapestry needle with a large eye, hand blanket stitch with yarn or heavy decorative thread, lightly encasing the raw edge of the fleece.

5. Remove the contrast basting stitches. For easiest removal, pull out the bobbin thread.

Double Layer Hand Blanket Stitch

The perfect finish on a traditional finish shawl collar, pocket, cuff, etc. The approach is the same as the raw edge blanket finish described on page 127 except that the blanket stitches are applied to the seamed and finished edge of the garment.

Using a shawl collar as an example:
1. The collar and facing have been sewn right sides together, trimmed, and turned to the finished position.
2. Machine baste a stitch gauge as described on page 127.
3. Hand blanket stitch with yarn, using a tapestry needle with a large eye.
4. Remove the basting stitches.

Plump-Edge Blanket Stitch

This is the same as the double layer blanket stitch except you "plump" the area encased by the blanket stitches.

Again, using a shawl collar as an example:
1. Sew the collar and facing right sides together.
2. When trimming, leave 1/2" seam allowance. Turn to the finished position.
3. Instead of using long contrast basting stitches for the blanket stitch gauge line, use shorter stitches and sew a permanent stitching line 5/8" away from the finished edge. Since this stitching will remain, use a thread color that matches the fabric.
4. Hand blanket stitch with yarn, using a tapestry needle with a large eye. Because the stitches are shorter, you will obviously count more stitches between hand stitches.
5. Do not remove the machine 5/8" stitch gauge line. The tightness of this stitching line combined with the bulk from the enclosed 1/2" seam allowance will plump the blanket stitched edge.

Diane Welch enjoyed finishing her plush mountain scene jacket with the traditional handstitched blanket stitch.

Serger Blanket Stitch

While not a true blanket stitch finish, this mock blanket stitch finish is fun for the serger junkie to play with.

Nancy's Note

All sergers are different. Experiment first on scraps of fleece, changing tensions until you achieve an acceptable appearance. Experiment on both the lengthwise and crosswise grain since they will react differently.

1. Remove the right needle for a wide three-thread stitch.
2. Set the stitch length and cutting width for the widest and longest stitch available.
3. Use Décor 6 thread in a size 100/16 needle.
4. When threading the needle, don't put the needle thread in the tension disc.
5. Use Woolly Nylon in both loopers and completely tighten both loopers.

Nancy's Note

These steps represent the starting point for adjusting your serger for a mock blanket stitch. Depending on the serger, you may have to modify these adjustments. If more looper tension is needed, hold the Woolly Nylon between your fingers.

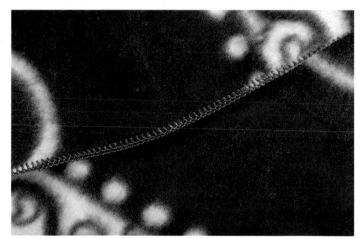

Chapter 9

SCRAP HAPPY

A Grab Bag Full of Ideas Using Small Pieces, Tidbits, & Scraps

Sewers and fleece are an environmentally friendly combination. Sewers hate to give up even the tiniest scrap of fabric if it can be used for something. And every scrap and tidbit of fleece can be constructively used, down to the last piece of fluff. Depending on how tenacious and determined you are to use every little bit, you may not even have to clean up your sewing area when finished! (Great! I'd rather sew than houseclean any day!)

Have fun with this chapter. There is nothing serious or profound here. Just a lot of potential for creativity, practicality, and fun. If you participate in holiday bazaars, you can even use some of these ideas to turn your leftovers into cash... And go buy more fleece!

Important Cutting Directions

Read this section before beginning any Scrap Happy project!

As you know, the right and the wrong sides of fleece react differently after wearing and laundering. Many fleeces are non-pill on the right side only. Since you will be working from your scrap heap, it is important to take the time to carefully determine the right and wrong sides of your scraps before sewing.

Most fleeces have more stretch on the crossgrain, from selvage to selvage, and less stretch on the lengthwise grain. Fleeces pulled on the crossgrain curl to the wrong side. (But you don't know where the selvages or crossgrain are because you are working with scraps! So...)

1. Pull the fleece in both directions to find the greater degree of stretch.
2. Pull the fleece across the direction of greatest stretch (that's the crossgrain).
3. Pulled on the crossgrain, the fleece will curl to the wrong side.
4. Using a Chacopel pencil, religiously mark the right side of your fleece scraps (mark the side opposite the curl).
5. Lay all your scraps right side up on the table before beginning any project.

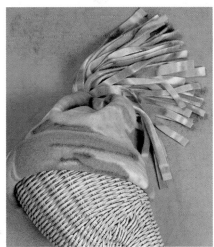

Meticulously following these easy steps will insure that you will always have the right side on the right side!

Nancy's Note

There are rare occasions where fleece does not follow this curl-to-the-wrong-side rule. Unless your fleece looks obviously better on one side than the other, follow the above steps.

Crusher Hat

(Blunt Edge Appliqué in Reverse)

You Will Need

❖ 1/4 yard each of two contrasting solid colors mid weight fleece (must have 25% stretch)
❖ Regular thread to match both colors

Crusher Hat Construction
(1/4" seam allowance)

1. From each fleece color, cut an 8¼" diameter circle for the top of the hat.

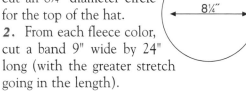

2. From each fleece color, cut a band 9" wide by 24" long (with the greater stretch going in the length).

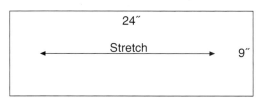

3. With right sides together, sew the short ends of each band together, forming a circle.

4. With right sides together and matching the center back seams, sew the bands together along one long edge. Turn right sides out.

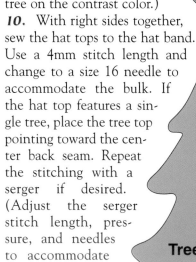

5. Using the tree template, outline straight stitch a tree at the center front of the hat band. Place matching threads in the needle and bobbin. (To determine the tree placement, roll back 3" contrast cuff. Place the top of the tree toward the finished seam. Unroll and stitch.)

6. On the contrast side, trim one layer only from the center of the tree.

7. Turn the band to the finished position (with the rolled-up cuff showing the tree and sides laying smoothly against each other). Trim approximately 3/4" from the top raw edge of the

outer layer to make the raw edges even. (The contrast color uses more than the main color in the roll-back.)

8. "Spot" baste circle hat tops with wrong sides together.

9. Outline stitch a single tree (or multiple trees) and trim one layer from the main color to reveal the contrast underneath. (The hat top shows a contrast tree on the main color. The hat band cuff shows the main color tree on the contrast color.)

Broken lines
show spot baste

10. With right sides together, sew the hat tops to the hat band. Use a 4mm stitch length and change to a size 16 needle to accommodate the bulk. If the hat top features a single tree, place the tree top pointing toward the center back seam. Repeat the stitching with a serger if desired. (Adjust the serger stitch length, pressure, and needles to accommodate the bulk.)

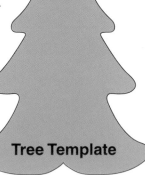

Tree Template

Fringed Scarf

You Will Need

➤ 1/4 yard each of two contrasting solid colors of mid weight fleece

➤ Regular thread to match each color

1. Place the scarves wrong sides together. Using a conventional sewing machine, stitch the long edges with a 1/2" seam allowance, leaving 5" unstitched at each short end for fringing.
2. Using a rotary cutter, trim to 1/4" away from the seamline.

3. Quick fringe 5" at each short end, making 1/2" cuts. (Refer to page 125 for quick fringe instructions.) Quick fringe both layers at once.
4. Using the tree template, outline straight stitch three trees staggered above the fringed ends at both ends of the scarf.
5. Trim one layer only from the center of the trees on one side of the scarf (revealing the contrast fleece).
6. Trim the opposite color at the other end of the scarf.

Fringed Scarf With School Spirit

A great gift for teens and college men and women! Choose the school's colors for each layer of fleece.

1. Stitch and quick fringe the scarf ends the same as above.
2. Using a collegiate or serif font from your computer, enlarge and print the school letters to fit proportionately between the 8" scarf seamlines. (A three letter sequence fills approximately 6" to 7" wide x 2½" to 3" high.)
3. Using a fabric marker or permanent felt tip pen, trace the outline of the letters on two pieces of Solvy (one set for each end of the scarf).
4. Lightly spray KK2000 on the Solvy and adhere it in place at each end of the scarf.
Caution: Plan first - you are reversing the colors at both ends. You will either adhere Solvy on opposite sides or flip the traced Solvy over before adhering.
5. Straight stitch outline the letters on the traced Solvy.
6. Remove as much Solvy as possible.
7. Trim one layer from the centers of the letters.

Mountain Scene Landscape

Thanks to Kathy Kleese for this magnificent mountain scene. Originally designed for UltraSuede appliqué, I revised it for Polarfleece blanket stitch appliqué. It's a terrific way to use scraps and leftovers while creating an eye-catching landscape appliqué. Use the landscape as a border along the lower edge of a jacket, pullover, tunic, or vest. Arrange it across the garment chest front. Place it across a jacket back. Or venture off into your own new territory and cascade mountains down from one shoulder.

This appliqué works best with mid-weight fleeces. The weights neither overpower nor underpower each other. When in doubt about how a particular fabric might work in your landscape, simply cut out the appliqué piece, spray it with KK2000, and temporarily adhere it in place. Hold up the garment and study if that area of the landscape caves in (too light in comparison to the rest of the scene) or buckles (too stiff in comparison to the other areas).

If combining other fabrics like flannels or woven cottons in your landscape, follow the appliqué method on page 100 for finishing the raw edges of those appliqué pieces. Choose a fusible interfacing that will help give the appliqué appropriate weight to balance with the other fleece appliqué pieces.

Avoid including the landscape appliqué in the garment hem. The resulting four layers of fleece would be too bulky. If you must include the landscape in the hem, eliminate one of the layers as follows:

1. Lengthen the landscape pieces 1½" at the bottom edges.
2. Trim 1" from the garment bottom edge.
3. When applying the appliqué pieces to the garment, extend the lower edge of the landscape scene 1" beyond the lower edge of the garment.
4. To hem the garment, wrap the extended 1" appliqué layer around the bottom cut edge of the garment, creating a 1" hem. (This nets out three layers of fleece.)
5. Topstitch the hem in place.

Depending on your color choices and whether you are a morning or a night person, your landscape appliqué can create the impression of a mountain scene at sunrise or sunset.

You Will Need

→ Fabric, ribbing, and notions for your base garment per the pattern requirements
    Color #1 fleece scraps (for 3 larger mountains)
    Color #2 fleece scraps (for 3 larger mountains)
    Colors #3 fleece scraps (for 3 smaller mountains)
    Color #4 fleece scraps (for 1 accent mountain)
    Fleece scrap for 3 suns (or moons)
    Fleece scrap for 1 cloud
    (Colors #3 and #4 can be the same or you can make all the mountains different.)
→ Sulky KK2000 temporary adhesive spray
→ Contrast rayon thread to blanket stitch appliqués (2 spools or 1 spool and 1 filled bobbin)
→ Appropriate needle for thread choice

1. Using the templates on pages 136-139, trace all the appliqué pieces on pattern tracing material or plain paper. Match continuation lines where indicated.
a) Continuation lines are indicated A - B - C - D.
b) The short broken lines denote the tracing and cutting lines for those appliqué pieces that underlap another appliqué piece. Be sure to include these extensions.
2. Lightly tape the paper scene together, creating one long mountain landscape.

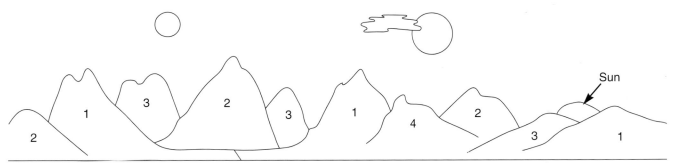

Sun

Left center front   Right center front

3. Measure the length of the mountain design and compare it to your garment's finished width measurement. Measure from the center front, around the back to the other center front.

4. Elongate or shorten the mountain scene as needed by lengthening or shortening mountain Color #2 at the left center front. If more length is needed, add to mountain Color #1 at the right center front (refer to the photo on page 134 of the finished scene). If making a larger size, add another mountain. For insurance, allow a little extra mountain length. Any excess can be trimmed off before adhering to the garment.

5. Cut out all the appliqué pieces. The numbers on the appliqué templates indicate the colors, not the order of stitching. (Be sure to read the Important Cutting Directions on page 131.)

6. If the garment has a center front opening, sew both garment side seams. If the garment is a pullover, sew one side seam.

7. Referring to the illustration of the finished scene, lay out the appliqué pieces accordingly. Be sure to overlap where indicated by broken lines. If the landscape borders a hemline, place the bottom edge of the scene 2" above the finished hem or ribbing seam.

a) If the garment has a center front opening, begin at the right center front and work around to the left center front.

b) If the garment is a pullover, decide what part of the mountain range you want at the center front and lay out the scene accordingly, beginning and ending at the open side seam. (*Hint:* Taping the traced appliqué pieces together may help determine placement.)

8. Following the blanket stitch appliqué directions on page 101, stitch the appliqué pieces in place. (Two contrast threads through the needle give a nice bold edge finish.)

9. Finish the garment construction. Since the side seams are already sewn, the order of sewing may vary slightly from the pattern directions. (If making a lined vest, the fat piping edge finish from *Adventures With Polorfleece* is an easy way to finish the armhole.)

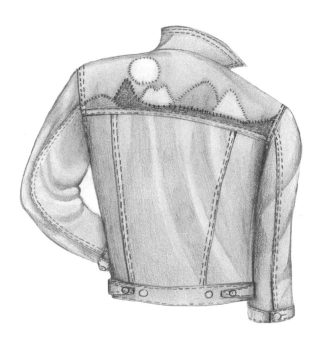

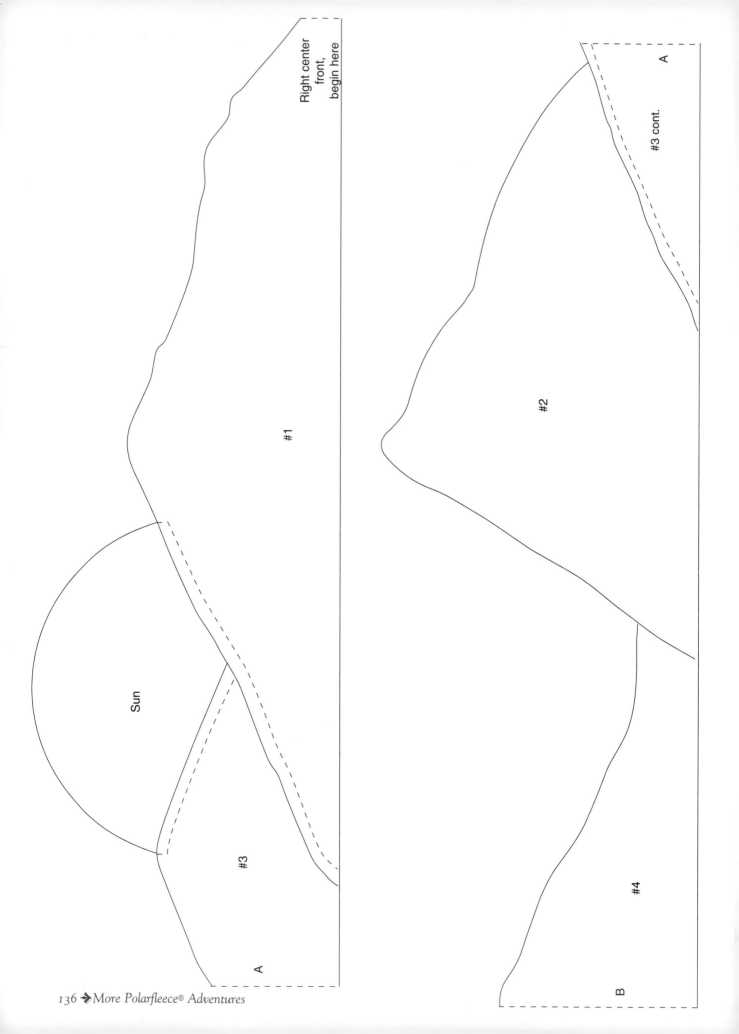

Right center front, begin here

#1

Sun

#3

A

#2

A

#3 cont.

#4

B

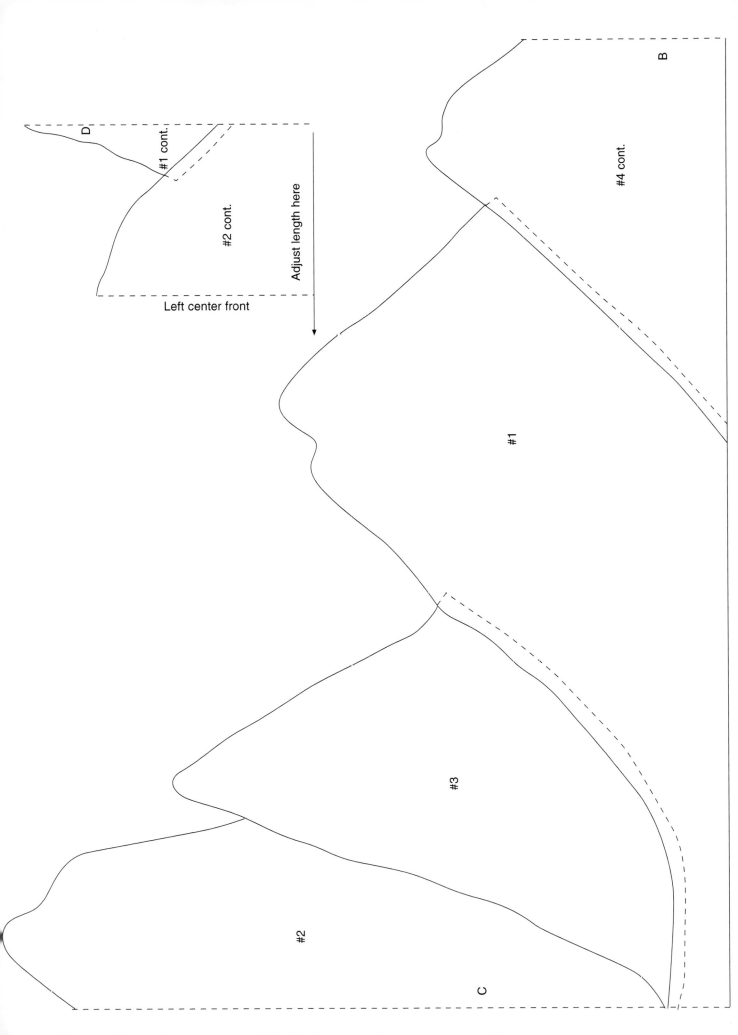

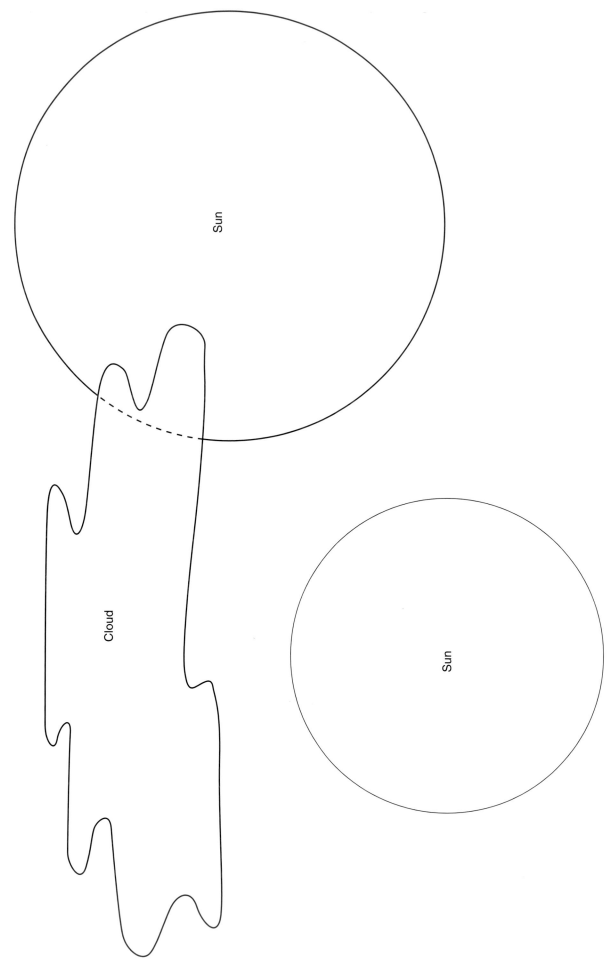

Sun

Cloud

Sun

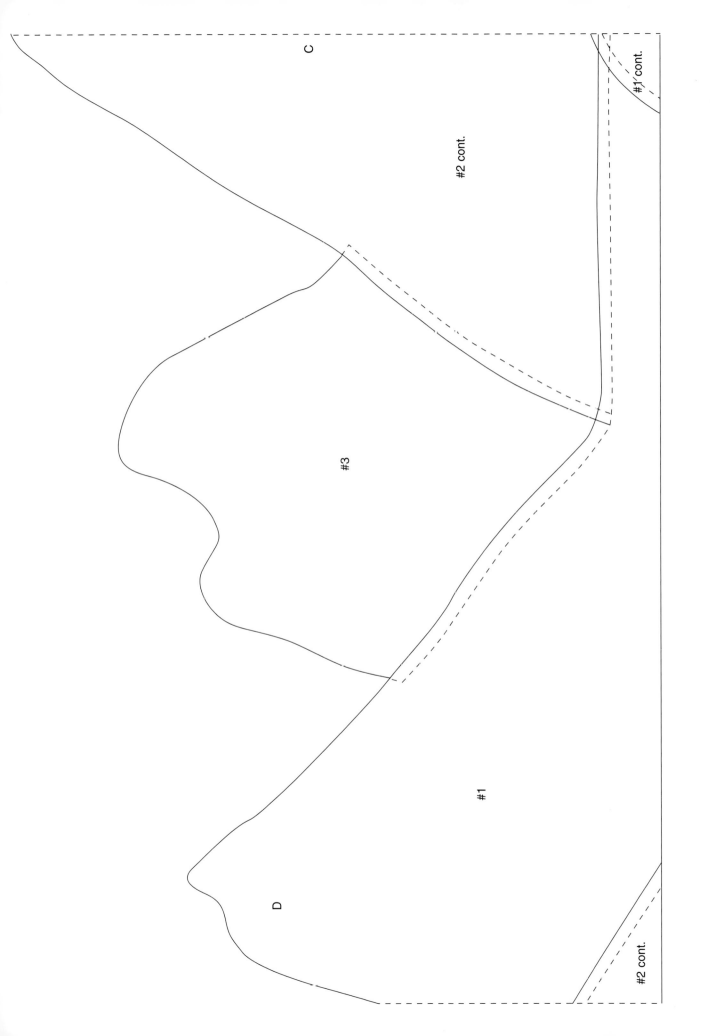

C

#2 cont.

#1 cont.

#3

#1

D

#2 cont.

Anything Goes Kid Jacket

Thanks to Julie Muschamp, a Northwest sewing instructor and designer, for sharing her clever use of leftovers in creating this designer jacket for her daughter Madison.

Since kids love bright colors and since color blocked outfits are more fun than "plain old solid ones," Julie took advantage of her Polarfleece stash to create this one-of-a-kind jacket.

Plan of Attack

Since multiple seam allowances from the smaller color block sections would be too bulky, Julie decided to butt the raw edges together and sew them together with a wide joining stitch. But, knowing this seam is not strong enough to withstand the rough-and-tumble lifestyle of a youngster...

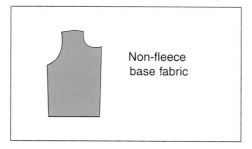

Non-fleece base fabric

1. Using your favorite pattern, cut out a jacket front, back, and sleeves from a non-fleece base fabric (woven cotton, muslin, flannel, interlock, etc.). You could choose a fabric to provide extra warmth if desired.
2. Play with your scraps and color block the garment pieces. You can plan and draw color block sections on your pattern piece or approach this step with the "crazy-patch" method.

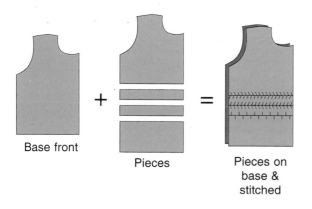

Base front + Pieces = Pieces on base & stitched

3. Butt the raw edges of the fleece together and lay it on top of the base fabric. When sewing the fleece pieces together with a wide joining stitch, the base fabric is incorporated in the stitching, lending strength and stability.

Julie's "I Refuse to Let Them Outgrow It Too Quickly" Trick

Kids tend to outgrow clothes in length quicker than they outgrow them in width. The first telltale sign of a growth spurt is the dreaded too-short sleeve.

When tracing the jacket sleeve pattern piece, add 3" to 5" extra length at the bottom hem. During construction, instead of sewing the usual hem allowance, turn up and sew the extra-deep hem. Turn back the sleeve hem for a roll-up cuff.

In the beginning, there is a nice full roll-up cuff. As the urchin sprouts, the cuffs get narrower, until eventually there is just a hemmed sleeve. Great idea for extended wear!

Mix 'n Don't Match Mittens

This idea is great for moms, grandmas, child care givers, or anyone who has lots of kids around, darting in and out with wet mittens. They come running in for lunch with wet soggy mittens and 15 minutes later they are ready to fly out the door again. Except their mittens are still soaking wet. Or they now have only one mitten for two hands!

Here's a terrific way to keep hands toasty warm and dry, maintain a large inventory of mittens, make good use of your polar scraps, and use those tidbits of stashed ribbing too small to use yet too large to toss out.

1. Have the kids trace around their hands on a piece of 8½" x 11" paper. (They love this part because now they are "helping you sew.") Then you draw another line, adding ½" or so wiggle room. Now you have a customized mitten pattern. (We aren't pretending this is high-tech. Just fun, practical, and cheap.)

2. Let the kids paw through your scrap pile and choose combinations of fleeces they like. Then let them paw through your "spare ribs" to pick ribbing for the cuffs.

3. Place two-somes of non-matching fleece scraps *wrong sides together.*

4. Using a rotary cutter (a wavy edge gives a fun edge finish), cut out lots of "custom mittens," cutting both layers at once.

5. Sew the mittens together by simply topstitching around the outer edges. Leave the blunt raw edges on the outside, don't sew and turn. If you want to get fancy, choose a stitch to mimic the fancy edge. The serpentine stitch complements a wavy edge. Use the multiple zigzag stitch alongside a pinked edge.

6. Cut ribbing cuffs and sew them to the mittens in the usual way (right sides together and turn).

The operative word here is "eclectic." Nothing matches. Nothing is supposed to! Fronts don't match backs (as a matter of fact, the shape of the front is exactly the same as the back so there really isn't a front and a back). The right hand doesn't match the left hand. Ribbing doesn't match anything at all!

The purpose is to let the kids reach in, grab two mittens at any time, and go outside to play! If they lose a mitten, nobody cares because it didn't match anything anyway! They are so fast and easy you can whip up a dozen in nothing flat.

No kids around? This is a great idea for a "Giving Tree," homeless donations, etc. And you feel good about using those leftovers. This is a win-win Scrap Happy project!

❧ Neck Gaitors ❧

These essential weather beaters are quick and easy to make while saving $20 to $30 over ready-made prices! Thanks to Jeanine Twigg from the Snap Source for her clever reversible "Snappy Neck Gaitors."

Here's a medley of neck gaitor ideas, all using pieces from your scrap stash. They are designed for fleece with moderate crossgrain stretch. Cut the gaitors with the greater degree of stretch going in the length (around the neck). These are not recommended for Berber or plush fabrics.

Single Layer Gaitor

1. Cut one gaitor 10" high x 21" long, with greater stretch going in the length.
2. With right sides together and using a 1/4" seam allowance, sew the short ends together to form a circle.
3. Turn under a 1/2" hem on both raw edges and top-stitch in place.

To wear: Slip the gaitor over your head and wear as a free-standing turtleneck to bridge the gap between your jacket neck opening and hat.

Double Layer Snappy Neck Gaitor Collection

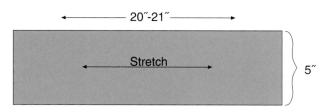

Idea #1: Finished Edges

1. Cut two gaitors 5" high x 20" to 21" long from coordinating fleeces, with greater stretch going in the length.

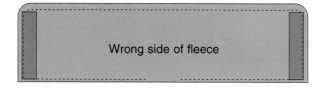

Wrong side of fleece

2. Gently curve the upper neck edge as illustrated.
3. On one gaitor, place 1¼" x 5" strips of non-fusible interfacing or muslin at each center front against the wrong side of the fleece.
4. Using a conventional sewing machine, stitch coordinating gaitors right sides together using a 1/4" seam allowance, catching the interfacing in the stitching. Leave an opening at the lower edge for turning.
5. Trim and grade the seam allowance to reduce as much bulk as possible. Trim the corners.

6. Turn the gaitors right side out and hand stitch the opening closed. Topstitch if desired.

7. Mark the placement for three size 20 sport snaps 1/2" from each center front. (This will result in a 1" overlap when snapped.)

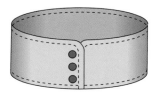
Finished edges

8. Attach sport snaps using the *decorative* caps on *all the snaps* (so when you reverse the gaitor, you have a pretty snap on both sides).

Idea #2: Blunt Edge Finish

1. Cut two gaitors 5½" high x 20" to 21" long from coordinating fleeces, with greater stretch going in the length.

2. Gently curve the upper neck edge as illustrated in the finished edge gaitor.

Blunt cut edges

3. On one gaitor, place 1¼" x 4 ½" strips of non-fusible interfacing or muslin at each center front against the wrong side of the fleece. Place the interfacing 1/2" from the cut edges of the fleece (so it won't show between the blunt raw edges on the outside of the gaitor).

4. Using a conventional sewing machine, stitch the gaitors together with *wrong* sides together, topstitching at a 1/2" seam allowance.

5. Using a wavy edge rotary blade, trim the outer edges of the gaitor 1/4" from the stitching line.

6. Mark the placement for three size 20 sport snaps 1/2" from each center front. (This will result in a 1" overlap when snapped.)

7. Attach sport snaps using the *decorative* caps on *all the snaps* (so when you reverse the gaitor, you have a pretty snap on both sides).

Idea #3: Blanket Stitch Edge Finish

Follow the directions for Idea #2: Blunt edge finish, except use a straight edge rotary cutter when trimming at step #4.

Hand blanket stitch all the raw edges before attaching the sport snaps.

Blanket stitch edges

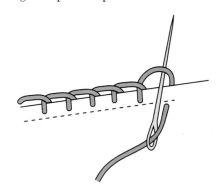

Polar Tam

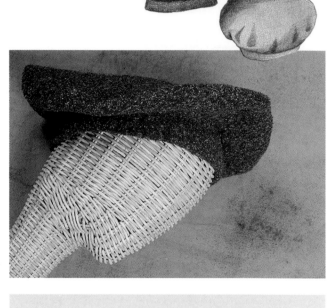

Make a quick, easy, and fashionable hat to coordinate with your favorite fleece jacket. Three pieces of fleece plus ten minutes sewing time and you are ready to put on your hat and go! This is designed for fleece with at least 20% (moderate) crossgrain stretch.

1. Draw a 13" circle for the tam top layer pattern. For the tam under layer, draw a 7" circle centered in the larger circle.

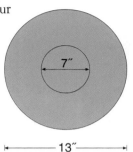

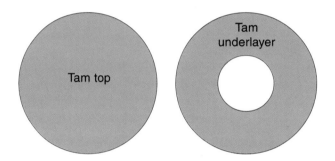

2. Cut 2 fleece 13" circles. Keep one circle whole for the tam top. Cut a 7" circle from the center of the second 13" circle for the tam under layer (like a donut).

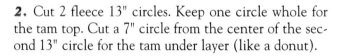

3. Cut 1 hat band 5" wide x 22" long, with greater stretch going in the length.
4. With right sides together and using a 1/4" seam allowance, sew the tam under layer (donut) to the tam top (circle) along the outer edges.
5. With right sides together, sew the hat band in a circle using a 1/4" seam allowance.
6. Fold the hat band in half, wrong sides together. Divide it in quarters and mark with pins.

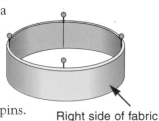

Right side of fabric

Nancy's Hint

Now is a good time to slip just the folded-in-half hat band on to see how you like the fit. If the fleece is quite stretchy, you might choose to make it a little smaller.

7. Divide the unsewn inner edge of the tam under layer (donut) in quarters and mark with pins.
8. With right sides together and matching the quarter divisions, sew the hat band to the tam under layer, using a 1/4" seam allowance.

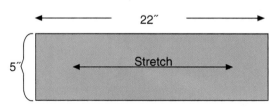

Wrong side of fabric

Nancy's Sewing Hint

Stitch with the hat band on the top and the tam under layer (donut) against the feed dogs. Ease the tam to fit the band or use your serger's differential feed.

9. Wear the hat with the hat band visible or tucked underneath.

Quick Fringe Hat

Designed for fleece with 25% crossgrain stretch.

1. Cut a fleece rectangle 22" high x 21" (small), 22" (medium), or 24" (large) wide, with the stretch going in the width.

2. Following the directions for quick fringing (page 125), make 1/2" cuts for fringe, 8" deep on one short end of the rectangle.

3. With right sides together, fold in half (22" x 10½", 11", or 12") and sew the center back seam with a 1/4" seam allowance, sewing from the unfringed short end and stopping at the fringe cuts.

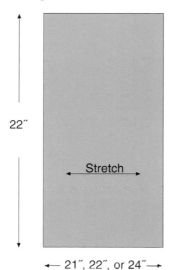

22″

Stretch

← 21″, 22″, or 24″ →

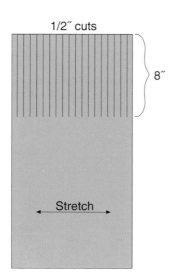

1/2″ cuts

8″

Stretch

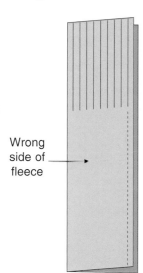

Wrong side of fleece

4. Turn up a 4" hem on the unfringed end and topstitch in place.

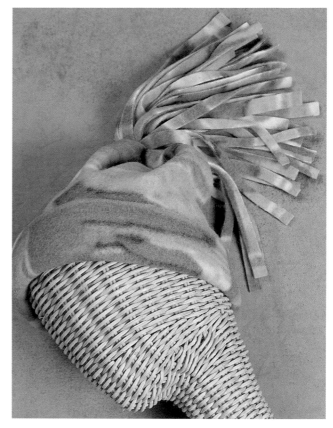

5. Cut a strip of fleece 1/2" x 22" for the fringed tassel tie. (Cut the tie on the straight-of-grain, resulting in very little stretch in the length of the tie.)

6. Tie the hat at the beginning of the fringe cuts to form a tassel at the top of the hat.

7. When wearing, turn up the hem for a rollback band.

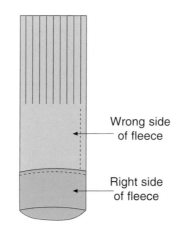

Wrong side of fleece

Right side of fleece

Finished view

*F*leece Shoulder Pads

As long as women have hips broader than shoulders…
As long as women have sloping shoulders…
As long as women have uneven shoulders…
As long as women want their clothes to hang better…

…Women will want shoulder pads to make their garments fit better and look better.

Tired of continually buying shoulder pads? Tired of continually changing shoulder pads from garment to garment?

Thanks to Michelle Stinson for this practical use of leftover fleece scraps.

1. Using the template, trace each shoulder pad layer on pattern tracing material.

2. Depending on the thickness of the fleece and the amount of shoulder padding you need, build your personalized shoulder pads.

a) If you need just a little overall padding, use two layers of E.

b) Build the shoulder pad, experimenting with adding and subtracting layers until you have just the dimension you need. There is no right or wrong. Everyone's needs and tastes are individual. Build the right pad differently than the left pad if needed.

c) Once you decide which layers to use, stack the layers on top of each other, graduating from smaller to larger, matching the shoulder notches

3. Lightly hand-catch stitch the outer curved edge of the smaller pad to the next larger pad (avoid dimples). Repeat until all the layers have been hand stitched together at the outer curved edges.

4. Trim off the shoulder notches.

5. Lightly whipstitch by hand the straight edges of the shoulder pad. Avoid compressing the fleece edge.

6. Place the shoulder pad in your garment with the largest layer next to the garment. Stitch the pad to the garment by hand-catch stitching a few stitches at the blunt (armhole) edge and at the curved (neck) edge. Or (if appropriate for your garment) machine stitch-in-the-ditch in the shoulder seam, sewing through the pad.

7. If the pad is too large, simply trim it at the outer edges.

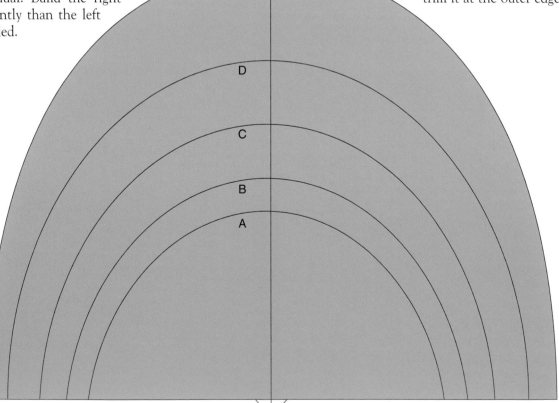

Jewelry Pouch

Long ago my mom gave me a lovely wrap-up jewelry pouch to organize and protect my jewelry when traveling. It is elegant velvet with satin lining and all sorts of zippered compartments. I love it and use it constantly. Looking at its simple design, I saw that it would be easy and practical to make from fleece. Since it is rolled up and tied closed, you can eliminate the tedious task of inserting all those tiny zippers.

1. Cut three 12" x 8" pieces of soft fleece (Layers A, B, and C).

2. Cut Layer A apart as illustrated.

3. Trim 1" from Layer B, making Layer B 11" x 8".

4. Keep Layer C whole.

5. Serger finish the top edges of pieces A1, A2, and A3.

6. With right sides facing up, lay piece A1 on top of Layer B. Stitch A1 to Layer B by stitch dividing A1 into two equal sections.

7. Lay piece A2 on top of Layer B, 1/4" away from the serger finished edge of A1. Stitch A2 to Layer B by edgestitching along the lower edge and by stitch dividing A2 into thirds.

8. Lay piece A3 on top of Layer B, 1/4" away from the serger finished edge of A2. Stitch A3 to Layer B by edgestitching along the lower edge and by stitch dividing A3 into thirds.

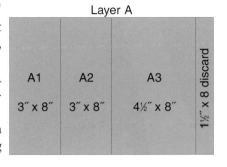

Layer A

A1 — 3" x 8"
A2 — 3" x 8"
A3 — 4½" x 8"
1½" x 8 discard

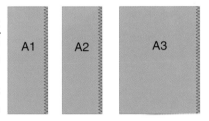

A1   A2   A3

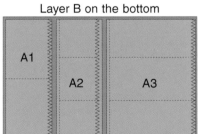

Layer B on the bottom

A1
A2   A3
1/4"   1/4"

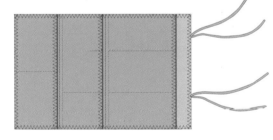

9. With wrong sides together, place the A/B Layer on top of the whole Layer C. Layer C will extend above Layer B by 1".

10. Serger finish the entire outer perimeter of the jewelry pouch. The top 1" will be finishing Layer C only, the rest will incorporate all three layers.

11. Cut two 30" pieces of ribbon or cording for the ties. Fold each tie in half and mark. Attach the halfway points of each tie to the single layer top edge of Layer C, 1½" from the side edges.

12. Insert your jewelry into the various large and small pockets. Roll up the pouch and tie to secure.

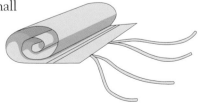

Golf Club Covers

Use leftover pieces of fleece to make soft cushioned club covers to protect your golf equipment. Choose either the regular or the extra-protection golf club covers. Extra-protection covers offer a long narrow ribbed cuff to protect graphite shafts.

Designed for medium to medium/heavyweight fleeces with little to moderate stretch. Since you will be sewing on four layers of fleece, use size 100/16 needles. (On heavier fleece you may even need to go up to 120/18 needles.)

Regular Golf Club Covers

Sew with a 1/4" seam allowance.

4¾"

Stretch

19"

11½"

1. For four club covers, cut from fleece:
a) For the tops: eight 4¾" circles
b) For the shafts: four 19" high x 11½" wide rectangles (greater stretch in the width)

2. If you wish to number the covers for individual golf clubs, use the templates on page 150 to appliqué 1, 3, 5, and 7 in the centers of four tops. (UltraSuede numerals edgestitched in place are classy.) Or use an embroidery machine to embroider the club numbers.

3. With wrong sides together, baste the pairs of circle tops together at the outer edges, resulting in four double-layered tops. Baste using a wide long zigzag stitch.

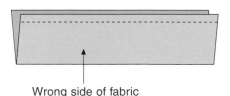

Wrong side of fabric

4. With right sides together, fold the shaft section in half (19" x 5¾") and stitch the long edge.

5. Fold the shaft section with wrong sides together (9½" high tube with the fold at one end and raw edges at the other, with the right sides of the fleece inside and outside of the tube).

6. Sew the circle tops to the raw edges of the tube end. If the top is numbered, place the number face down (facing inside the tube) and place the seam at the top of the number.

7. Turn the golf club cover to the finished position.

Raw edges, 2 layers

Folded edge - double layer of fabric right sides facing inside and outside

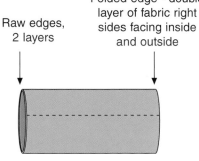

Fleece right side out

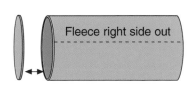

Graphite Shaft Golf Club Covers

Similar to the regular golf club cover except that the fleece portion is shorter and extends into a long ribbed cuff to protect the graphite shafts. For the ribbed cuffs, you will need a heavyweight ribbing (soft spun nylon is good), or sweater ribbing that will offer cushioning. If the ribbing is 26" or wider, you will need 22" of yardage. If narrower, you will need 44" of yardage.

Sew with a 1/4" seam allowance.

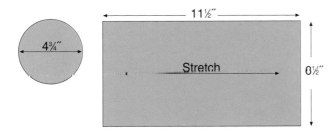

1. For four club covers:
a) For the tops: cut eight 4¾" fleece circles.
b) For the shafts: cut eight 6½" high x 11½" wide fleece rectangles (greater stretch in the width).
c) From heavyweight ribbing, cut four cuffs 22" high x 6½" wide (greater stretch in the width)
2. If you wish to number the covers for individual golf clubs, use the templates on page 150 to appliqué 1, 3, 5, and 7 in the centers of four tops. (UltraSuede numerals edgestitched in place are classy.) Or use an embroidery machine to embroider the club numbers.
3. With wrong sides together, baste the pairs of circle tops together at the outer edges, resulting in four double-layered tops. Baste using a wide long zigzag stitch.
4. Fold each of two fleece rectangles in half with right sides together (to measure 6½" x 5¾") and sew a tube.

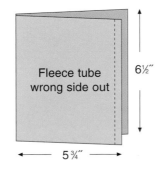

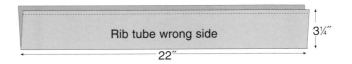

5. Fold one ribbing piece in half (22" x 3¼") and sew the long edges to form a rib tube.

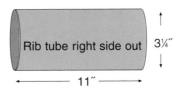

6. With wrong sides together, fold the rib to finished position, forming a rib cuff (11" high).

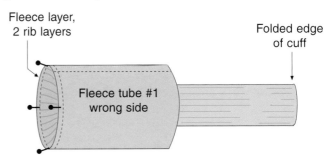

7. With right sides together and matching seamlines, use a conventional sewing machine to sew the ribbing cuff to a single fleece tube, stretching the ribbing to fit. An easy way to do this is to have the fleece tube wrong side out. Insert the ribbing cuff inside the tube and sew both ribbing raw edges to the raw edge of the fleece tube. Leave in this position for the next step.

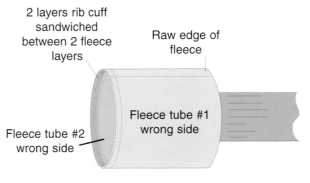

8. Insert the second fleece tube into the ribbing cuff, with the right side of the fleece against the ribbing, and again sew the raw edges together. The net result is a double layer rib cuff sandwiched between the right sides of both fleece tubes.

9. Turn the fleece tubes right sides out. Double check to make sure the double layer fleece tube has raw edges at one end and the finished rib cuff at the other end.

Fleece top,
numbered side down

Fleece tubes
right side out

Rib cuff right side

10. Sew the basted circle tops to the fleece tube raw edges. If the top is numbered, place the number face down (facing inside the tube) with the seam at the top of the number.

11. Turn the golf club cover to the finished position, pulling the fleece tube through the ribbing cuff.

Is your golfer constantly searching for a ball marker? Attach a small UltraSuede V flap on each club cover and affix a couple sport snaps. The colored snap caps make terrific ball markers!

Dog Overcoat

Thanks to Phyllis Elfers and her "best friends" Jake and Kurby for this clever way to keep shorthair dogs warm on those chilly daily walks. Jake and Kurby are Australian Shepherds who appreciate the extra warmth these overcoats provide. I was trying to design a Canine Cover-Up for this book when Phyllis helped me with her idea.

Not only can you save almost $100 (ready-made cost), you can custom fit your dog and make the coat appropriate for your climate. Make it with two layers of fleece. Or with fleece backed with heavy flannel for more warmth. Consider making the inner layer from fleece for warmth and the outer layer from water repellent fabric for rainy weather. Add a thermal batting layer between your fabric choices for more warmth.

Don't have a piece of leftover fleece large enough? Not to be defeated… color block one!

The Small, Medium, Large, and Extra Large sizes on page 152 can be used as is, or as starting points to custom fit your furry friend.

You Will Need

→ Fabric (for each layer):
  Small: approximately 10" x 13"
  Medium: approximately 16" x 20"
  Large: approximately 22" x 28"
  Extra Large: approximately 26" x 33"
→ 1 to 1½ yards 2"-wide, medium firm elastic
→ 9" to 15" 1½"-wide Velcro
→ 2 yards reflective tape (optional)

1. On pattern tracing material, use the gridded pattern on page 152 to draw the size closest to fitting your dog.
2. Compare your dog's center back neck-to-tail measurement with the traced measurement. Lengthen or shorten as necessary. The coat should end at the base of the tail.
3. Lay the traced pattern on your dog's back. The sides of the coat should end around the mid-chest area. The neck extension should lay smoothly around the sides of the neck. (The extensions don't meet at the center front, they will fasten with Velcro tabs sewn on elastic.)
4. At the coat center back, tail end, pinch 1" of fabric and baste it in a 1/2" pleat on both layers of fabric. (This provides a slight bit of shaping.)
5. Using a 1/4" seam allowance, sew the coat layers right sides together, leaving a small opening for turning.

6. Turn the coat to the finished position and hand stitch the opening closed.
7. Topstitch the outer edges if desired.
8. Topstitch reflective tape around the outer edges or in a decorative design if desired.

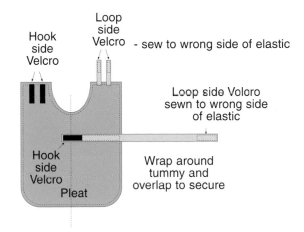

9. For the "belly belt," measure the dog's tummy at the fullest part. Cut elastic this measurement plus 6" (for edge finishing and overlap).
10. Refer to the illustration and lay the elastic belly belt in place. The position is approximately 1/4 of the center back measurement away from the neck.
11. Turn the elastic raw edge under 1/2", sandwiching it between the coat and elastic and stitch in place.
12. Stitch along both long edges of the elastic, securing the elastic to the coat.
13. On the coat end of the belly belt, center and stitch in place a piece of Velcro (hook side) 1½" x 3" to 5" long (3" for smaller dogs, 5" for larger dogs).
14. On the free end of the belly belt elastic extension, turn the elastic under 1/2" and stitch to finish.
15. On the underside of the elastic extension, stitch the companion piece of Velcro (loop side), covering the raw stitched edge of the elastic.
16. Refer to the illustration and sew 1½" x 3" to 5" Velcro pieces (hook side) to the left front. (Small dogs only need one piece of Velcro.)
17. For the right front, attach two elastic extensions 4" to 7" long (depending on dog size), finishing the elastic ends the same as for the belly belt. (Small dogs only need one 3" elastic extension.)
18. Sew 1½" x 3" to 5" Velcro pieces (loop side) to the wrong side of the elastic extensions.

Now that your loyal friend has been patiently waiting while you sewed, dress him (or her) in his new overcoat and take him out for a well-deserved walk!

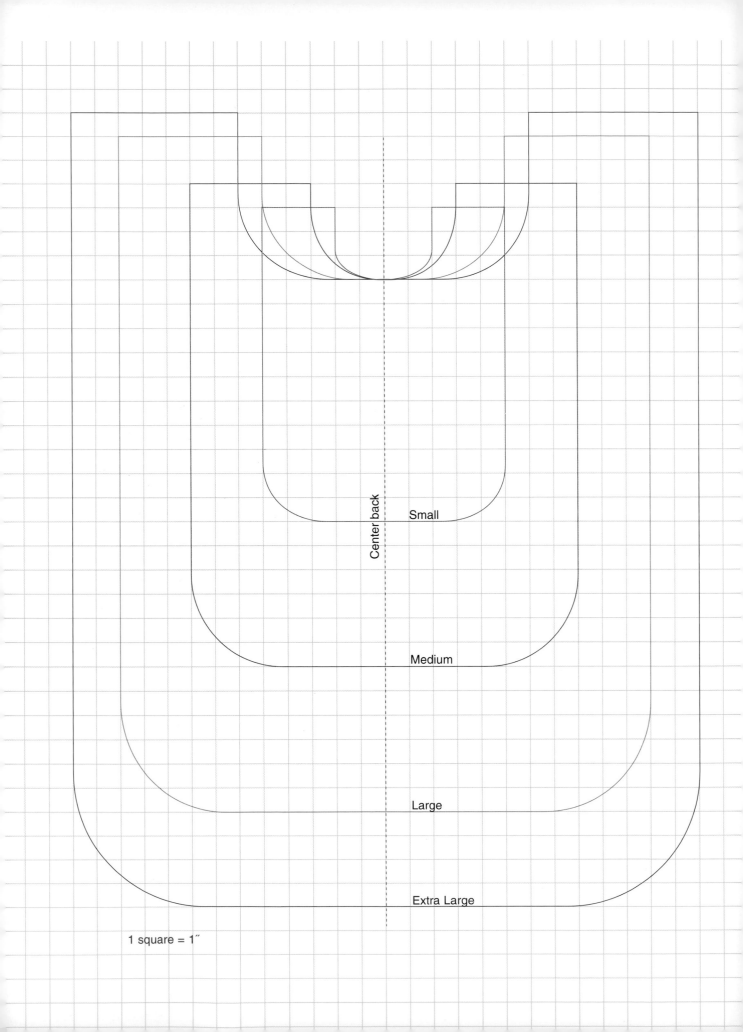

Center back

Small

Medium

Large

Extra Large

1 square = 1″

After Thoughts

An assortment of "ditsy" ideas for using leftovers creatively and practically. These didn't warrant a category all their own, but were too good (and too much fun) to ignore. Every scrap is usable!

Snake Draft Stopper

Another clever idea from Phyllis Elfers. Use your scraps to make a friendly patchwork fleece snake to block out the drafts at the base of the door. When not stopping the cold, coil him up to serve as a conversation piece.

1. Cut your scraps (even tossing in some tighter knitted Berber scraps) into 6" x "whatever-you-have" lengths (irregular lengths from 3" to 6" are good).

2. Sew them end-to-end, making one long (minimum 40") strip.

3. Fold in half (to 3" x whatever length). Stitch across one short end and down the long edge. (If you want to add a little character and charm, appliqué eyes and a mouth before sewing the patchwork tube. A slip of ribbon makes a great tongue.)

4. Turn the tube right side out.

5. Fill with kitty litter, rice, pellets, etc. and sew the open end closed.

6. Enjoy your new "keeper of the cold."

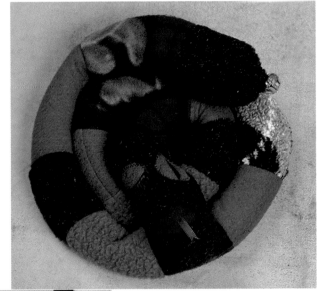

Thanks go to Phyllis Elfers for this clever use of leftover pieces of fleece. When the weather is mild and calm, coil this multicolored snake and place him on the hearth. When the winds howl, put him to work as a door draft stoppter.

Wrist Snuggies

Another clever problem-solver found in your scrap pile. Wrist snuggies are long, single-layer cuffs that tuck into the top of your gloves and up into your coat sleeve, covering that vulnerable often exposed wrist area. Ski clothing addresses this problem, but regular everyday coats and gloves frequently leave a couple inches of skin exposed to the cold.

Simple solution: sew a pair of wrist snuggies from scrap fleece!

1. Cut two pieces of fleece 7" high x your loose wrist measurement plus 1/2" (loose enough to slip your hand through). Place greater degree of stretch going around the wrist.

2. Form a cylinder and sew with a 1/4" seam allowance. (Make sure the stretch is going around the wrist.)

3. Now you can walk the dog or shovel the snow without chaffed wrists.

Wineglass Panty

Like your wine ice cold, but not the drips from the condensation? Put "panties" on your wineglass!

1. From fleece, cut two circles 1/2" larger than your wineglass base. For a blunt edge finish, a wavy edge rotary blade is nice.

2. Cut one circle in half across the middle.

3. Place the cut circle on top of the whole circle and stitch together 1/4" around the outer edges.

4. Insert a wineglass into the slit opening and enjoy dry tables!

2 layers of fleece with stitching

Slit opening

Motif Shaped "Panty"

Remember this snowflake print from earlier chapters? A leftover snowflake motif makes a lovely coaster. Wrong sides together, outline straight stitch the motif to plain fleece. Cut the excess away and slit the opening for a wine glass.

Stuffed Toys

Fleece makes great stuffed animals. Soft. Cuddly. If stuffed with fleece scraps, they can be easily tossed in the washer and dryer to launder. If you don't have a favorite pattern, let your fleece print help you.

1. If using an animal print, cut out the animal motifs and edgestitch them together (see blunt edge finish on page 122), leaving an opening for stuffing. Stuff with fleece scraps and stitch the opening closed.

2. No suitable motif? Make a crescent shape, heart, ball, or cube.

3. Want a little noise? While stuffing, insert a child-proof prescription bottle that contains one or two dried beans. It provides a nice, mellow rattle sound. Thanks go to Martha Maurer for this idea.

Sunglasses Holder

Tired of constantly losing and re-buying sunglasses holders? Now if you lose one, you can whip up another in five minutes!

1. Using a wavy edge rotary blade, cut two fleece rectangles 3½" x 7", gently rounding the corners.

2. Edgestitch three sides at 1/4", stopping 1/2" shy of the left-open end.

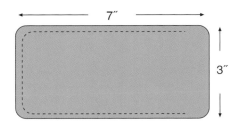

Pet Pillow Bed

This clever idea is a "groaner." One of those ideas where you think, "How obvious! I could have thought of that myself."

The respectable sized scraps of fleece get tossed into your "Scrap Resource Center" for appliqué and various small projects. But there are always bits and pieces that you know you'll never use. Too small. A print scrap not suitable for small usage. Whatever. Don't toss those… Recycle them into a soft, cushy pet pillow bed! When it needs to be freshened up, simply toss in the washer and dryer.

Look at your favorite furry friend and determine what size polar pillow would make a good size bed for him. Fluffy the cat will be enthralled to curl up on a 12" to 18" pillow. Medium-sized Rover would expect a 20" to 26" cushion, while Brutus will demand a larger throne, probably 30" to 36". (If you want to get fancy, you could create a curved or ball-shaped design like those found in catalogs retailing for $40 to $60.)

1. Cut two layers of fleece, Berber, or plush fabric in the bed size you need.

2. With right sides together, sew three of the sides, leaving one short end open.

3. Make a loop from twill tape or draw cord and attach it to the open short end of the bed.

4. Hang the loop on the doorknob of your sewing room door.

5. As you sew all your fleece projects, toss all the leftover unusable bits and scraps into the open end. (This saves sewing area clean-up time too!)

6. When it's as full and fluffy as you want, remove the loop, sew the short end closed, and present it to your faithful companion.

Between the Scrap Happy chapter and the closing pet pillow bed idea, your scrap heap should be pretty well depleted and your sewing room should have relatively little clean-up. (Theoretically, maybe not in reality!)

And so we have come to the end of another fun-filled Polarfleece adventure. I hope you've had as much fun reading and trying my ideas as I've had writing them for you.

Keep Warm and…

Happy Sewing!

About the Author

Nancy Cornwell, also affectionately known as the "Polar Princess," is an avid sewer and designer and recently became an award-winning author when her *Adventures With Polarfleece* was selected as the PRIMEDIA 1998 Sewing Book of the Year.

Garment design has long been a passion of Nancy's. She enjoys redesigning commercial patterns to reproduce ready-to-wear garments and create new designs. Rarely does she construct a garment from a pattern without a few tweaks and enhancements to make it her own.

Nancy loves to share her ideas, techniques, and love of sewing with other sewers. Her fun and enthusiastic approach to sewing is infectious and inspires confidence in sewers of all levels. An accomplished speaker, teacher, and lecturer, Nancy regularly makes presentations to sold-out audiences for consumer groups, sewing exhibitions, television sewing programs, and industry events across the country. For the past 15 years, she has been the featured speaker at the Sewing & Stitchery Expo, the largest home sewing consumer event in the nation.

Nancy's love and expertise on sewing with fleece comes from living in the Pacific Northwest where the lifestyle is casual and outdoorsy. She and her husband Jeff have owned a Stretch & Sew Fabrics retail fabric store for 18 years, where the focus is on better casual and sportswear fabrics. Nancy's love of fleece makes sewing an ongoing adventure!

Index